St. John of the Cross

for Beginners

Also by William Meninger

Julian of Norwich: A Mystic for Today
(Lindisfarne Books, 2010)

St. John of the Cross

for beginners

WILLIAM MENINGER, OCSO
ST. JOHN OF THE CROSS

LANTERN BOOKS • NEW YORK
A Division of Booklight, Inc.

2014
LANTERN BOOKS
128 Second Place, Brooklyn, NY 11231
www.lanternbooks.com

The Ascent of Mount Carmel and
The Dark Night of the Soul are paraphrased
for this book by the author from several sources.
Cover and text design: William Jens Jensen
Cover image: *View of Toledo* by El Greco (1596–1600)

❧

LIBRARY OF CONGRESS CATALOGING-IN-PUBLICATION DATA

Meninger, William.
 St. John of the Cross for beginners / William Meninger, OCSO.
  pages cm
 ISBN 978-1-59056-463-9 (pbk. : alk. paper) —
ISBN 978-1-59056-464-6 (ebook)
 1. John of the Cross, Saint, 1542–1591. Noche oscura del alma.
 2. Mysticism—Catholic Church. I. Title.
  BV5082.3.J643M46 2014
  248.2'2—dc23

                                                    2014023721

Contents

THE ASCENT OF MOUNT CARMEL: BOOK THE THIRD

THE DARK NIGHT OF THE SOUL: BOOK ONE

THE DARK NIGHT OF THE SOUL: BOOK TWO

INTRODUCTION

St. John of the Cross, Juan de Ypes y Alvarez, was born in 1542 of Jewish ancestry, in the town of Fontiveros near Avila, Spain. He died, aged 49, in 1591. His father had married beneath himself and was disowned by his family. He and his wife supported themselves by weaving until he died when John was only seven. His mother, Catalina, took John and his brothers to Medina del Campo where she was able to eke out a living. One of John's brothers died soon after, probably of malnutrition. He received a rudimentary education at a poor children's school, later studying the humanities with the newly founded Jesuits while he worked with the poor. In 1563 he entered the Carmelite Order and one year later was sent to the prestigious University of Salamanca for studies. He was ordained a priest in 1567. Soon after that he met St. Teresa of Avila who persuaded him to join her in the reform of the Carmelites.

The success of the reformed Carmelites met with considerable opposition from the friars and nuns who had no desire for reform. The apostolic delegate and King Philip II favored the reform and John, who was very successful in working for it, was caught in the crossfires between them and his former superior. John was actually arrested by the unreformed friars and for nine months, until he escaped, enduring great suffering and privations. He was publicly flogged before the community once a week, was confined to a tiny cell with little light and was given a starvation diet. Strangely enough it was during this captivity that he produced some of his greatest poetry.

After his escape his time was chiefly taken up with the foundation and government of new monasteries. After the death of Teresa of Avila in 1582, he once again fell under the crossfires of opposing factions within the order, was deprived of his offices, and banished to one of the poorest monasteries of the order, where he fell seriously ill. He was granted literally the opportunity to follow his own advice to "suffer and be despised." However, before his death, his sanctity was acknowledged even by his enemies, and his funeral was the occasion of great religious enthusiasm. He was canonized in 1726.

Like St. Teresa of Avila, St. John of the Cross seems to have found his inspiration for his teachings on mystical theology from his own experience. He knew the Scriptures by heart and was well versed in the teachings of St. Thomas Aquinas. However, there seems to be little influence from the great European and English mystical writers. In his *Ascent of Mount Carmel,* John of the Cross teaches, evidently from his own experience, that the soul must empty itself of itself in order to be filled with God. It must be purified through purgation and suffering from every trace of earthly dross in order to be fit for a blessed union with God. He reveals to the soul, seemingly complacently traveling along the road to union, a variety of imperfections of which it was completely ignorant. These must be eliminated by way of active purgations before the soul is then called to the Dark Night, a condition of heavy, passive, interior trials with their direct origin in God. The soul is now passive but not without its own role in embracing the divine mercies showered upon it, even though with much suffering. The soul emerges finally from the dark night and enters into the bright day of God's light, sharing in his divinity, as described in the *Spiritual Canticle* and the *Living Flame of Love,* neither of which is for beginners.

THE ASCENT OF MOUNT CARMEL: BOOK THE FIRST

The nature of the dark night and how necessary it is to pass through it to divine union, and especially the dark night of the sense and desire.

PROLOGUE

To explain the dark night through which the soul must pass in order to attain perfect union with God insofar as it is possible in this life, four things are necessary. One must have knowledge, experience, understanding of the Scriptures, and fidelity to the sound teachings of the church. Many souls, when they set out upon the spiritual journey and are graced by God to do so, make no progress. They must allow themselves to be led by God through a dark night of trials and aridity, temptations and hardships. They make no progress because they do not desire to enter into this dark night or because they do not understand themselves or because they lack competent spiritual directors to guide them.

Sadly, many souls who are called by God to a deep communion of love never achieve this. There is no one to show them the right path or to teach them how to go from the beginnings of the spiritual life into the darkness that must be traversed in order to experience the dawn of God's love. Inadequate spiritual directors actually hinder God's grace and at times, through their ignorance and poor advice, delay progress or prevent it altogether. They may even tell the soul under their care that they are suffering from a psychological issue, not a spiritual one, or that they simply have a morbid personality or some hidden sin that they do not wish to deal with.

Some people themselves are the cause of their problems. These are people who don't really know themselves, who lack the virtue of humility, that is knowledge of the truth about themselves. They think that by their own efforts they can make this journey toward union with God. They are like naughty children who, when they need to be carried, fuss and struggle to be allowed to walk on their own. As a result they make no progress or proceed at a child's pace.

This book is intended to show everybody, both beginners and proficients, how to commit themselves to God's guidance. They must allow God to lead them into that dark night and on that difficult and troublesome road to divine union. Too often people think that these necessary trials are due to their own fault and so they just increase their own difficulties. Sometimes, too, false directors, thinking that trials proceed from sin, crucify the soul afresh by making them re-examine their lives and make general confessions which are not suitable for the state they are in. They should really be encouraged and comforted to accept their condition until God is pleased to do otherwise with them.

With God's help, we will look at the signs that will tell us whether a soul is undergoing the dark night and whether it be the dark night of the sense or of the spirit, or some psychological problem or even some hidden sins. There are many other things on this road that may happen to those who follow it, both consolations and desolations, some coming from the guiding hands of God and others from our own imperfections. This book is not for souls who wish to travel toward God by pleasant and delightful ways. It will provide solid and substantial instruction for those who desire to pass through those detachments, both temporal and spiritual, which hinder their union with God.

CHAPTER 1

THE DARK NIGHT

For the soul to attain to the state of perfection, ordinarily it must pass through two principal kinds of night, which are actually purgations or purifications of the soul. We will call them nights because the journey through these purgations and purifications is, as it were, by night in darkness.

The first purgation is the dark night of the senses. The second purification is the dark night of the spirit. In both cases, it is the soul that undergoes the dark night but through its different parts, the sensual part and the spiritual. The night of the senses pertains to beginners and occurs when God begins to bring them into the state of contemplation. The night of the spirit or purification pertains to those who are already proficient and occurs when God wishes to bring them to a higher state of union.

In the dark night of the senses the soul is called forth by God out of love for him to a privation and purgation of all its sensual desires—that is, to all physical things of the world appealing to the flesh and to the desires of the will. Unless our desire for worldly things is mortified and put to sleep, we will not be free. This mortification is difficult. It is a dark night, but it is also a blessing. We cannot do it of ourselves but only with the help of God.

~

Chapter 2

DARK NIGHT OF THE SENSES

The soul must gradually deprive itself of the desire for all worldly things. This can only be done with God's help by denying these things to oneself. This is, as it were, a dark night to all of our senses.

There is another darkness through which the soul must travel. This is faith, which is dark as night to our understanding. A third darkness has to do with the goal of our journey; namely, God. In this life, God is equally a dark night. The soul must pass through these three nights or, if you wish, these three parts of one dark night. It is by means of the night of the spirit, which is faith, that the soul passes into the third night in which God communicates himself by faith to the soul in a secret manner that becomes another night to the soul. This night is far darker than the others are and is followed by a complete union with the Wisdom of God who is Jesus.

Actually, these three parts of the night are all one night but in the manner of night it has three parts. The first part, which is that of the senses, may be compared to the beginning of night, to evening, the time when all things begin to fade from sight. The second part, which is faith, can be compared to midnight, or total darkness. The third part, which is like the end of the night, is God and is near to the light of day.

CHAPTER 3

A FURTHER LOOK

Let us consider now the night of the senses. Here the soul is deprived of the pleasure of its desire in everything. The soul remains, as it were, unoccupied and in darkness. The philosophers tell us that as soon as God infuses the soul into the body it is a blank tablet. There is nothing upon it and nothing can come upon it until it is experienced through the senses. The five senses are like windows of the soul. Only the five senses can imprint anything upon this blank tablet of the soul. Absolutely nothing is communicated to it in this life in the course of nature from any other source.

So if the soul rejects and denies everything that it can receive through these senses it remains, as it were, in darkness and empty. It is true, however, that the soul continually exercises its faculties of hearing and seeing and smelling and tasting and touching. It does this automatically and all of the time. This does not matter, for if the soul denies and rejects the objects of senses, it is not hindered by them even if they are continuing to operate. We are not speaking here of the lack of things. But if the soul has a desire for them it is not detached. We are speaking of detachment from the things of the senses because this is what leaves the soul free and empty of them even though it still possesses them. These sensual things, these things of the world, do not in themselves occupy the soul or cause it harm since they do not really enter it. What dwells within the soul is the will and the desire for sensual things. This is what harms the soul and must be mortified. The principles herein stated are almost universally accepted. They play a strong role in the spirituality of all the great religions.

By way of a brief review then, we have said that the soul has two parts—a sensual part and a spiritual part. These are the equivalent of two dark nights; one is a dark night of the senses in which the desire of the soul is mortified and detached from all sensible things of the world, the other is a dark night of the spirit in which the soul must proceed by faith alone, being mortified and detached from even spiritual things. This is followed by a kind of third night that is proximate to a deep union of God insofar as it is possible in this life. This is a night because God must always remain hidden in a kind of darkness while we live. It is the night, however, which is closest to the dawn. We will now examine further the dark night of sense.

CHAPTER 4

THE NECESSITY FOR THE DARK NIGHT OF SENSE

The soul must pass through this dark night of the mortification of the desires and pleasures of material things because the affection that it has for them is equivalent to darkness in the eyes of God. When the soul has these affections it has no capacity for being enlightened by the simple light of God because light cannot agree with darkness.

Affection for creatures is darkness, and affection for God is light. These two have no likeness and the light of divine union cannot dwell in the soul if these affections are not mortified. Let us look into this further.

The attachment that the soul has to creatures renders the soul like to these creatures, and the greater the attraction, the closer is the resemblance between them. Love is an equalizer and sometimes it can even demean the lover. A man who has a great attachment to rich foods, in spite of the fact that they may be very unhealthy for him, demeans himself and lowers himself from the status of a noble, intellectual creature formed in the image of God to an animal lusting for material pleasure. So he that loves a creature becomes as low as that creature and even in some ways lower. So it is that the soul loving anything less than God becomes incapable of pure union with God and bonds as an equal with some creature.

Take the example given by Julian of Norwich. She saw all beings divided into two; God and God's creation. She was given to see God's creation, as it were, like a hazelnut in the palm of her hand. It was so frail she thought it would go out of existence, but God assured her that his love would sustain it. Nevertheless, she realized that to give oneself to anything less than God is the equivalent of giving oneself to a hazelnut. When you give yourself to a creature rather than to God, that is what you will get, basically—a hazelnut.

Compared to God all creatures are nothing, and the soul that sets its affection on creatures will be unable to comprehend God until it be purged of them.

If all the beings of creation, compared with the infinite being of God, are nothing, then the soul that sets its affection upon them is likewise nothing in the eyes of God. That which is not can have no communion with that which is. The beauty of creatures compared with the beauty of God is nothing, and the soul attached to creaturely beauty cannot be attached to God. Indeed, the soul that sets its affection upon any of the good things of the world in and for their own sake cannot set its affection upon the good things of God. Even the wisdom of this world is foolishness with God. We must lay aside this wisdom to acquire the true wisdom that is God. In order to come to union with the wisdom of God the soul has to proceed by unknowing all that its mind can know. This is mortification and the dark night indeed.

The soul that is enamored of worldly office, worldly honor, and worldly esteem is a base slave and a captive. Slavery can have no part with liberty and liberty cannot live in a heart subject to desires. This is the heart of the slave, not of a child of God. All of the delights and pleasures that the will can take in things of the world in comparison with the delights that are found in God are affliction, torment and bitterness. One that sets one's heart upon them is worthy then of affliction, torment and bitterness, and will be unable to attain the delights of embracing union with God.

~

CHAPTER 5

NECESSITY FOR THE DARK NIGHT

The distance between what creatures are in themselves and what God is in himself is infinite. Souls that set their affection upon any of these created things are therefore placing themselves at an infinite distance from God. This applies to the desire for all things natural or even supernatural. This is why Jesus told us that we must renounce everything we possess in order to be his disciples. The soul has no capacity to receive transformation in the Spirit of God unless it rejects all lesser things. God gave the children of Israel the food from heaven, the manna, only when the flour that they had brought from Egypt failed them. The food of angels is not fitting for the palate that finds delight in the food of humans. We must reserve our desires exclusively for God alone. The soul that wishes to love some lesser thing together with God makes little account of God for it weighs in the balance against God something that is infinitely removed from God. Any soul that journeys on the road or climbs the mountain to God must be careful to mortify its desires. The sooner it does this, the sooner it will reach the end of its journey, the summit of its mountain. Otherwise it will never reach it. Even the practice of the virtues will not avail it because it will be unable to attain to perfection in them. This can only be done by purifying the soul of every desire.

The soul must do three things to ascend the mountain of God. First, it must cast away all affections and attachments to anything less than God. Second, it must purify itself of even the remnants these desires have left in the soul by means of the dark night of the senses—that is, by habitually denying them and repenting of them. Third, through its observance of these first two things God will transform it, give it a new understanding of himself and a new love of God in God. Being stripped of its old desires the soul will now be brought into a new state of knowledge and delight. Old images and forms of knowledge will be cast away and all that belongs to the natural sense will be clothed with a supernatural aptitude with respect to all its faculties. Knowledge will become wisdom. What was its human operation will become divine and the soul will become an altar whereupon God alone is adored in praise and love. It is only when no other love is mingled with it that the soul may be a worthy altar. God wills that the soul should have only one desire, which is to do his will perfectly and to bear upon oneself the cross of Christ.

Chapter 6

Two Serious Evils

Desires for anything but God are the cause of two serious evils in the soul: they deprive it of the spirit of God, and the soul is wearied, tormented, defiled, and weakened.

The more the soul is given to affection for a creature, the more the desire for that creature fills the soul, and the less capacity it has for God. Two contrary things cannot be contained within one will—affection for creatures and affection for God. For what has the creature to do with the creator, the sensual with the spiritual, the visible with the invisible, the temporal with the eternal, food that is heavenly and spiritual with food that is of the senses. As long as the soul is subjected to the sensual spirit, the pure Spirit cannot enter it.

All created things are merely crumbs that have fallen from the table of God. This is the food of dogs. It will never satisfy the soul but only whet its hunger. It is the nature of the soul who has these desires that it is always discontented and dissatisfied. What has the hunger that all creatures suffer to do with the fullness that is caused by the Spirit of God? Fullness, which is uncreated, cannot enter the soul unless it first casts out that created hunger which belongs to sensual desire. Two contraries, hunger and fullness, cannot dwell in one person.

God created the soul from nothing. How much greater is his work in the cleansing and purging of these contradictions. They are more completely opposed to God and offer him a greater resistance than does nothingness, for nothingness resists not at all.

The desires for creatures also wearies the soul, torments it, defiles, darkens and weakens it. Desires weary and fatigue the soul. They are like restless children who are always demanding this or that from their mother and are never content. They are like water disturbed by the winds, never allowed to rest in any place or in anything. They are not filled by the satisfaction of their desire because they feed on that which can only cause them greater hunger.

Chapter 7

Desires Torment the Soul

The soul which is given to sensual desires is not only wearied and fatigued, but also is tormented and afflicted. It is like a captive bound with cords from which it has no relief. This is what concupiscence does. It afflicts the soul and gives it no relief. The more intense the desire, the greater the torment it inflicts upon the soul. The bonds with which it is bound are its own desires. Let the soul remember the promise given through Isaiah: "Let all who thirst come to the waters, and all that have no silver of your own buy from me and eat; buy from me wine and milk without the silver of your own will and without giving me any labor in exchange for it." He promises to give rest to our souls and relieve them from their heavy burdens because his yoke is sweet and his burden is light.

❧

CHAPTER 8

DESIRES DARKEN AND BLIND

E
ven as fog darkens the air and obscures the bright sun, so the soul that is clouded by desires is darkened in its light—that is, its understanding. It allows neither the sun of its natural reason nor that of the supernatural wisdom of God to shine upon it. Such as a soul is not only darkened in its understanding but it is numbed in its will and memory. These faculties depend upon the understanding and become dull and disordered when its light is impeded. The understanding loses its ability to receive enlightenment from the wisdom of God, the will loses the power to embrace God in pure love, and the memory is clouded by the darkness of desire and is unable to take clearly upon itself the form of the image of God.

Desire of itself is blind and depends upon the understanding that leads it as a child leads a blind man. It has no understanding in itself, so when it is guided by itself it becomes the blind leading the blind. Concupiscence dazzles the understanding and until the dazzling power of desire is taken away it will be blinded.

It is useless for the soul to burden itself with extraordinary penances and many other voluntary practices thinking that this will suffice to bring them to the union of divine wisdom. This will be of no avail unless they diligently work to mortify their desires. One month of mortifying the desires is worth many years of penances. The darkness of the soul will remain until its desires are quenched.

If we only knew how great is the blessing of Divine Light of which we are deprived by the blindness that proceeds from our affections and desires! If we only knew what great evils we fall into day after day so long as we do not mortify those desires! The soul must not think that it may indulge in its affections and desires and still rely upon its clear understanding or upon the gifts it has received from God. The soul will be blinded and darkened and fall even more. Remember how Solomon, the wisest of men, was reduced to such blindness and torpor of the will so as to make altars to idols and worship them himself because of the affections he had for women. In his old age his desires blinded and darkened his understanding and succeeded in quenching that great light of wisdom which God had given him.

CHAPTER 9

DESIRES DEFILE THE SOUL

We would do well to note here that the teachings of John of the Cross regarding the desires for sensual things and their harmful effects must be correctly understood. We all desire sensible things and probably always will. God created the senses and the objects of the senses and, like all things, in creation he saw that it was good. When John of the Cross refers to the desire for sensual things he means desiring them to the exclusion of God, desiring them for their own sake. Everything in creation is given to us as a manifestation of God and as a means toward attaining union with God. It is when this means becomes an end, when we desire sensual things for their own sake and to the exclusion of their purpose in leading us to God. By and large, St. John of the Cross seems to avoid the word "sin." This, however, is what he means when he refers to our desires for sensible things.

A warning must be given here. Sometimes souls are misled by an inadequate understanding of John of the Cross' teaching on the dark nights. They tend to see the normal trials—burdens, sufferings and crosses that afflict every soul—as signs that they are in the dark night. They even use this as an excuse for not dealing with these trials through the normal, healthy, human means at our disposal, whether medical or psychological. Physical or mental illnesses, postpartum depression, midlife crises, social or economic reversals are seen as dark nights of the sense or the spirit. This, at times, may be true for some or all of these things but it is not true in the normal course of human events. The dark night of the sense comes about through graced choices the soul makes to mortify freely the desire for sensual pleasures. The dark night of the spirit comes about passively through the action of God in souls that have passed through the night of the sense and are living in the total darkness of faith. This should not be confused with melancholy or depression. A dark night that is led by faith is never without hope. People who experience depression that is totally devoid of any form of hope are suffering from a serious psychological illness that even includes thoughts of suicide. This should be dealt with by professional help.

A further evil that these desires cause in the soul is that they stain and defile it, as we are taught in Ecclesiastes, "He who touches pitch shall be defiled with it." The soul touches pitch when it allows the desire of its will to be satisfied by any creature. Thus something that is beautiful becomes stained and defiled. A soul is in itself a lovely and perfect image of God but just as traces of soot would defile a lovely and perfect face, so would disordered desires defile the soul that has them. In its natural being the soul is good as God created it. But in its reasonable being, without reference to God, it can be vile, abominable and full of evil. Even a single unruly desire that is clearly not a mortal sin is enough to bring the soul into such a bondage and foulness that it can in no way come to union with God until it be purified. If this be so with one desire, imagine what impurities a variety of desires will cause in the soul. One single disorder of the reason can be the source of many different impurities. Through uprightness of the soul, the righteous man has one single perfection that results in innumerable gifts of the greatest riches and many virtues of loveliness, each one different and full of grace according to its kind. So the unruly soul, according to the variety of desires which it has for creatures, has in itself a miserable variety of impurities. The understanding, the will and the memory are all corrupted by these desires. So any unruly desire, even for the smallest imperfection, stains and defiles the soul.

❧

CHAPTER 10

DESIRES WEAKEN THE SOUL IN VIRTUE

Desires harm the soul by making it lukewarm and weak so that it has no strength to pursue virtue or to persevere in it. The more desires the soul has, the more its strength is dispersed. If the desire of the will is spread among many things besides virtue, it must be weaker as regards virtue. The soul that is not recollected in one single desire for God loses strength in the pursuit of virtue. It is like an un-pruned tree whose strength is sapped by superfluous shoots. Such desires may kill the soul and even if they don't reach this point, they make it unhappy with regard to itself, unfruitful with respect to its neighbors, and weary and slothful with respect to the things of God. The soul is given a strong distaste for following virtue when it is consumed by desire for creatures. The reason many souls have no eagerness to gain virtue is that they have affections which are not pure and not fixed upon God.

CHAPTER 11

FREEDOM FROM DESIRES

Must the soul undergo total mortification in all its desires, great and small, or may it simply mortify some of them and keep others that may seem insignificant? It is true that all voluntary desires are not equally harmful. We do not speak here of natural desires which hinder the soul very little from attaining union when they are not consented to. To mortify them completely in this life is impossible. A person may well experience such desires and yet be quite free from them according to his or her rational spirit. It may even happen that in deep, wordless prayer these desires may be dwelling in the sensual part of the soul, and yet the higher part has nothing to do with them.

All of the voluntary desires, grave, venial or only imperfections, must be driven away, however slight they be, if the soul is to come to this complete union with God. Divine union consists in total transformation of the will according to the will of God. There must be nothing in the soul that is contrary to God's will. In this union, the will of God and the will of the soul are one.

It is written that the just man shall fall seven times a day, but he is still a just man. This kind of fall is not voluntary and proceeds from natural desires that are unintentional. However, habits of voluntary imperfections, which are never completely conquered, prevent Divine Union and progress in perfection.

I speak here of habitual imperfections, such as gossiping or some slight attachment to a person, an article of clothing, a book, or a particular kind of food. To become habitually attached to things like these (their number is legion) is of great harm to the soul's progress in virtue. Even if the imperfection is extremely slight, progress in perfection will not be possible. A bird can be held from flying by a strong string or a thick rope. The result is the same; it is held down. Even if the soul possesses much virtue, it will not attain to the liberty of divine union if it clings to imperfections.

What a pity it is that God often grants souls strength to resist strong temptations but they fail in the blessing of divine union because they have not shaken off some childish thing that God had bidden them to conquer for love of him. Not only do they make no progress, but also because of this attachment they lose that which they have gained and retrace that part of the road along which they have traveled at the cost of so much time and labor. On the spiritual journey the soul either goes forward or goes backward. "He who is not with me is against me." A great fire comes from a single spark. One imperfection is sufficient to lead to another, and yet to another, and many more arising from the same weakness. We have seen many persons to whom God has been granting the favor of leading them a long way into the spiritual journey and yet by merely beginning to indulge some slight attachment, under the pretext of doing good, or in the guise of conversation and friendship, lose their spirituality and their desire for God and holy solitude. Thus one imperfection leads to another, and this leads to yet more. Many desires arise from one weakness or imperfection caused by these desires. Souls whom God has been leading a long way into the spiritual journey through some slight attachment under the pretext of doing good, or in the guise of conversation and friendship, often lose their spirituality and their desire for God and holy solitude.

We must constantly be mortifying our desires. The soul has only one will, and that will, if it be compromised by anything, is not free and pure, which is necessary for divine transformation. If these desires are not mortified, we fall into them and go from bad to worse. St. Paul says in his letter to the Corinthians II: Brothers, the time is short. It behooves you that they who have wives should be as if they had none; and they that weep for the things of this world, as though they wept not; and they that rejoice, as if they rejoiced not; and they that buy, as though they possessed not; and they that use this world, as if they used it not! This shows us how complete our detachment of soul must be from all things if it is to journey to God.

CHAPTER 12

WHAT ARE THESE DESIRES?

Can just any desire be sufficient to work these evils in the soul and deprive it of the grace of God? Desires that would deprive the soul of God can only proceed from voluntary desires that are mortal sins. They deprive the soul of grace in this life and of glory in the next. Any desire, however, great or small, is sufficient to produce in the soul blindness, torment, impurity, weakness, etc. Desires which are mortal sin produce total blindness, weakness, torment, etc. Lesser desires do not deprive the soul of grace but do produce these negative defilements depending upon the nature of the desire.

An act of virtue produces in the soul sweetness, peace, consolation, light and fortitude. But an unruly desire causes torment, fatigue, blindness and weakness. All the virtues grow through the practice of any one of them, and all the vices grow through the practice of any one of them likewise.

Once again it must be observed that we do not speak here of natural desires which are not voluntary or temptations to which the soul is not consenting. Temptations are never sins and even though the soul who suffers them may think that they produce in it defilements and blindness, this is not the case. In fact, they are bringing it the opposite advantages. Insofar as the soul resists them, it gains all the opposite virtues. Virtue is made perfect in weakness.

CHAPTER 13

THE WAY TO ENTER THE NIGHT OF SENSE

The soul enters the night of sense in two ways. One way is active, the other passive. The active way consists in that which the soul does of itself to enter the dark night. The passive way is that wherein the soul does nothing but God works in it. Here, only patience is required. It will be well to set down briefly here the way which is to be followed to enter this night of the senses. The counsels given here for conquering the desires are few and concise and adequate for one who sincerely desires to practice them.

Let the soul have an habitual desire to imitate Christ in everything. Let it meditate on the life of Christ so it may know how to do this in the manner of Christ. Let it renounce every pleasure that presents itself to the senses if it be not purely for the honor and glory of God. The soul must never desire any sensual thing for its own sake. It must not desire the pleasure of looking at things unless this helps it Godward; in its conversation let it also act this way. And so in respect to all the senses insofar as it can, the soul must avoid the relevant pleasures. If this is not possible, it must at least desire not to have it. In this way it will soon reap great profit.

The soul must strive to embrace with all its heart the following counsels so that it may enter into complete detachment with respect to all worldly things for the sake of Christ. Try to prefer not that which is easiest but that which is most difficult. Seek not that which gives the most pleasure but that which gives the least. Choose not that which is restful but that which is wearisome. Look not for that which is greatest, loftiest and most precious but for that which is least, lowest and most despised. Strive to go about seeking not the best of temporal things but the worst. If this is done with a full heart, the soul will quickly find in them great delight and consolation.

If these things be faithfully put into practice, they are quite sufficient for entrance into the night of sense. For greater completeness, however, let us look at another exercise that will help us mortify those things that reign in the world and from which all other desires proceed; namely, concupiscence of the flesh, concupiscence of the eyes and the pride of life. Let the soul strive to work, to speak and to think humbly of itself and desire all others to do so.

The following advice is given here in reference to the night of the sense but it will later also be applicable to the night of the spirit. In order to have pleasure in everything, desire to have pleasure in nothing. In order to possess everything, desire to possess nothing. In order to be everything, desire to be nothing. In order to know everything, desire to know nothing. This does sound very harsh and difficult, but the proof of it is in the experience of those who have done it. Their yoke is sweet and their burden is light.

When your mind dwells upon anything, you are ceasing to cast it upon God who is everything. To arrive at the All, you must deny yourself everything. When you possess the All you must possess it without desiring it. In this kind of detachment, the spiritual soul finds its repose, for it covets nothing, and nothing wearies it. This is not something that can be accomplished by human effort, but only through the grace of God.

❧

Chapter 14

The Effects of the Dark Night of the Sense

For the soul to conquer the desires and to deny itself the pleasures that it has in things, it needs to realize and experience that there is a greater love and a greater enjoyment. This comes from setting its desire on God and deriving from Him its pleasure and strength. The sensual part of the soul is attracted towards sensual things, so the spiritual part then must be enkindled with greater yearnings for that which is spiritual to allow it to throw off the yoke of nature and enter this night of sense. Remember here that night of sense means an absence, a mortification, a denial of sensual desire. The soul needs this greater yearning for spiritual desires so it will have the courage to remain in this dark night of the sense and its deprivations. All the trials and the perils of this dark night are made easy and sweet by the soul's desire for its Spouse. All of the labor and all of the mortifications the soul employs to abandon its own self will, during this night of the senses, prove to be a joy to them.

~

CHAPTER 15

RELEASE FROM CAPTIVITY

On account of the human condition (Original Sin), the soul is a captive, subject to the passions of human nature with its bondage and subjection. To go forth from this condition without being impeded by it is a great blessing. When this finally happens, the self-will (sensual desire) is at rest. It is, as it were, lulled to sleep through the mortification of our sensual nature. This is necessary so that the soul may go forth to true liberty and to union with its Beloved.

❧

THE ASCENT OF MOUNT CARMEL:
BOOK THE SECOND

CHAPTER 1

THE SECOND PART OF THIS NIGHT

The soul now moves on from stripping itself of all sensual imperfections to stripping itself of all desires for the possession of even spiritual things. It is much more difficult to put to rest the spiritual part of the soul and its desires and to enter into this interior darkness (the dark night of the spirit), which is a spiritual detachment from all things, whether sensual or spiritual, and leaning on pure faith alone. This is the ascent of Mount Carmel, the ascent to union with God. It is an ascent of faith and the soul has to remain in darkness as to all light of sense and understanding. It must go forth beyond all limits of nature and reason to attain to the heights of God. Because it ascends by faith, the soul is clothed with the Divine. In this condition, its own reason does not recognize it nor does the devil. These things cannot harm one who journeys in faith. The very darkness of faith conceals it from all sources of harm.

This part of the journey is exceedingly secure for the soul because it does not depend upon its own sight. Rather it is like a blind person having for a guide supernatural Faith. Its sensible impulses and yearnings, its natural faculties, and its spiritual and rational parts have been lulled to sleep. The soul has no more yearnings. It needs no more than a denial of all faculties and desires of the spirit in pure faith. When this is attained, the soul is united with the Beloved in a simple and pure likeness.

The darkness of the spiritual night is far greater than that of the night of sense. It is even more than a night; it is darkness itself. However dark a night may be, some light can always be seen, but in true darkness nothing is seen. This spiritual darkness, which is faith, takes away from the soul everything that it might understand and that it might sense. Nothing is seen. The soul does not move forward under its own power but only with the power of God.

Chapter 2

The Darkness of Faith

Faith is the wonderful means by which we are led to our goal, which is God. God is the goal, or the third part of this night. Faith is the means to God and is compared with midnight, the darkest time of the night. The night of the sense was compared to the beginning of night, when sensible objects can no longer be seen, but it is not as far removed from light as is midnight. The night of the spirit is the darkest; it is midnight. The third part of the night, just before dawn (which is God), is close to the light of day, and therefore not so dark as midnight. Here God begins to enlighten the soul by supernatural means which is the beginning of perfect union and which, while it is still done in faith, can be said to be less dark.

The night of the spirit has an active part and a passive part. We must see how the soul has to prepare itself actively to enter into this night. The passive part, which God will work in it, will be treated later.

CHAPTER 3

FAITH IS A DARK NIGHT TO THE SOUL

Faith, according to the theologians, is a habit. It is both certain and obscure. It is an obscure habit because by it we believe truths revealed by God that transcend all natural understanding. Paradoxically, the excessive light of faith is a thick darkness. Just as the sun overwhelms all other lights, so faith overwhelms greater and lesser things. The light of faith transcends the faculty of intellectual vision and disables the understanding because the understanding extends only to natural knowledge.

By him- or herself one only knows after a natural manner; that is, things that one attains by means of the five senses. One only knows objects which present themselves to the senses. Things beyond one's understanding whose likeness one has never perceived would give one no illumination whatever, no knowledge at all. Can a person born blind really understand what color is?

So it is with faith. It tells us of things which we have never seen or understood. So we have no natural knowledge concerning the things of faith. We hear about them and believe what we are taught. We bring our natural understanding into subjection to what we hear. Faith comes from hearing. It is not knowledge that enters by the senses, but is only the consent that the soul gives to what we hear. Things that we believe by faith are not illumined by our understanding, which has been rejected for the sake of our faith.

Obviously then, faith is a dark night for the soul, a dark night which paradoxically gives the soul light, light it could not have in any other way. The more the soul is darkened, the greater is the light that is given to it.

CHAPTER 4

THE NEED FOR THIS DARKNESS

In order to be guided by faith, the soul must not only be in darkness with respect to its sensual part involved with creatures and temporal things, but also it must be blinded and darkened according to that part which has involvement with God and spiritual things.

We are speaking now of supernatural transformation. The word "supernatural" refers to that which soars above the natural self, which remains beneath it. The soul's activity here is to completely and voluntarily empty itself of anything that can enter into it by way of its affection and will. When the soul does this, it is resigned and detached and even, we might say, annihilated. If even the tiniest bit of self-will remains, the soul will wander off following its weak and misguiding light. It is only when nothing of the self remains that God is free to accomplish his will in the soul without hindrance. The soul that would be joined in a union with God must not walk by understanding, nor experience, nor feeling, nor imagination. It must have faith in God's Being, which is not perceptible to the understanding, experience or imagination. In this life the highest thing that can be felt or experienced concerning God is infinitely removed from God. Eye has not seen, nor ear heard, nor has it entered into the heart of man what God has prepared for those who love him. However much the soul may desire to be perfectly united through grace with God in this life, it must be in darkness with respect to everything that can enter through the senses, which can be imagined with the fancy or understood with the heart. Should the soul cling to any of these things it will be greatly impeded from reaching union with God. God lies beyond all these things, even the highest that can be known or experienced. God can only be known by unknowing.

To go to God, the soul must travel on a way that has no way. In this state there are no longer any ways or methods. Actually, the soul has within itself all ways after the manner of one who possesses nothing yet possesses everything. The soul then must pass beyond all that can be known and understood, both spiritually and naturally. It must desire to come to that which in this life cannot be known, or sensed or imagined. It is only by leaving behind everything that it is able to experience and feel in this life that it will desire that which surpasses all feeling and experience.

For the soul to be free to do this it cannot cling to anything it receives, either sensually or spiritually. The more emphasis the soul puts on what it understands, experiences and imagines, and the more it esteems these things, the more it loses of the supreme good and the more it is hindered. However, the less it thinks of what it may possess in comparison with the highest good, the more it dwells upon that good and esteems it. This approach is done in the darkness of faith that, in a wonderful way, actually gives to the soul the true light. This comes from the Father of lights, and not from the soul itself, which remains in darkness.

The "Cloud of Unknowing" advises us to be wary of consolations, sounds, joys, or delights originating from external sources. They may be either good or evil, the work of a good angel of the work of the devil. "But if you avoid vain sophistry and unnatural physical and emotional stress, it will not matter if they are good or evil, for they will be unable to harm you." Our source of authentic consolation is the "reverent, loving desire that abides in a pure heart" (Chapter 48).

CHAPTER 5

THE UNION OF THE SOUL WITH GOD

God dwells in and is present substantially in every soul, even in that of the greatest sinner. This is how God preserves them in being. If such a union were to fail them, they would be annihilated. So when we speak of union of the soul with God, we speak not of this substantial union which is continual, but of the transformation of the soul with God, which is not being brought about continually but only when that likeness which comes from God is produced. That union by which we are preserved in being is called substantial and is a natural union. The union of which we speak is called a union of likeness and is supernatural. The supernatural union happens when the soul's will and the will of God are conformed together as one and there is nothing in the soul's will repugnant to the will of God. When this happens, the soul is transformed in God through love.

Since no creature whatsoever, and none of its actions or abilities, can conform to that which is God, the soul must be stripped of all things created and of its own actions and abilities; namely, it's understanding, perceptions and feeling. When all that is unlike God is cast out, the soul may receive the likeness of God. Nothing will then remain in it that is not the will of God and it will thus be transformed into God.

This kind of supernatural union is communicated only by love and grace, which is certainly not possessed by every soul. In addition, those souls that do possess it do not have it in the same degree. Some have a greater love than others.

This is what is meant by being born again in the Holy Spirit. It means having a soul like God in purity, having in itself no admixture of imperfection, so that pure transformation can be brought about in it. The soul and God are one. The soul is God by participation. What God is by his essence the soul becomes by grace. It may be compared to a window completely without the tiniest spot of dust marring its surface. The sun shines through this window and, while the window remains a window, it is indistinguishable from the rays of the sun.

The preparation of the soul for this union is not in understanding, feeling, or imagining anything concerning God. It does not come about that way but only through perfect resignation and detachment from everything for God's sake alone. When a soul, according to its greater or lesser capacity, does attain to union this union will depend upon what the Lord is pleased to grant. For some souls it is greater, for some it is lesser. Each soul is satisfied according to its capacity, even though some may be many degrees higher than others are.

CHAPTER 6

THE THREE THEOLOGICAL VIRTUES

The three virtues of faith, hope, and charity cause emptiness or darkness in the faculties of the soul. Faith causes emptiness in the understanding, hope causes emptiness in the memory and charity causes emptiness and detachment in the will.

Faith tells us what cannot be understood with the understanding. It is the substance of things that appear not. It brings certainty to the intellect but not clearness; rather it brings obscurity.

Hope renders the memory empty and dark. Hope always relates to that which is not possessed for if it were possessed, there would be no more hope. Hope that is seen is not hope. So this virtue then also produces darkness. In a similar way charity causes emptiness in the will with respect to all things. It obliges us to love God above all things. This cannot be done unless we withdraw our affection from them in order to set it holy upon God. He who does not renounce all that he possesses cannot be my disciple, Jesus tells us. Thus all three of these virtues leave the soul in obscurity and emptiness in respect to created things.

These three virtues then inform the three faculties of the soul: faith, hope, and love inform understanding, memory and will. Each of these three faculties must be stripped and set in darkness concerning all things except these three virtues. These are the three theological virtues and, unlike any other virtues, can only come from and lead to God. God is their beginning, God is their means, and God is their object or goal.

The virtue of faith must inform the intelligence. The virtue of hope must inform the memory. The virtue of love must inform the will. There is no room for anything else save only these three virtues. This is the night of the spirit. It has an active and a passive aspect. This aspect is active because the soul does everything that it can to enter into the night by voiding the faculties of all other objects or, at least, the desire for all other objects except for God.

There is a method by which we can do this. By this method we can empty the intelligence of everything except faith in

God; we can empty the memory of everything except hope in God; we can empty the will of everything except love for God.

The crafts of the world, the flesh and the devil are many and devious. The power of self-love is subtle and deceptive. Spiritual persons who do not know how to become detached and govern themselves according to these three virtues can be hindered and deceived. However, when they follow this method they will have complete security against these crafts and this self-deception. I am speaking especially to those who have begun to enter the state of contemplation, those who are going beyond the ways of prayer that call for the exercise of thoughts, words, images, and desires and are entering into the repose of God's presence in darkness.

CHAPTER 7

THE NARROW WAY

In the Gospel of St. Matthew, chapter 7, Jesus tells us how straight is the gate and how narrow the way that leads to life; and how few there are that find it. By saying how straight is the gate, he is speaking of the night of the senses and how the will must be detached from all things temporal, and God must be loved above them all. By saying how narrow is the way, he is saying the soul has also to disencumber itself completely in regard to those things which pertain to the spirit. The way of perfection is a steep and narrow road and requires travelers who have no burdens weighing upon them with respect to sensible things or spiritual things. Even among spiritual persons, there are not many who are willing to do this. Many are called but few are chosen.

To instruct us and lead us into this road, our Lord gives us, in the eighth chapter of St. Mark's Gospel, a wonderful teaching, encouraging us to disencumber the soul from everything that belongs to creatures or to the spirit. "If any man will follow my road, let him deny himself and take up his cross and follow me. For he that will save his soul shall lose it; but he that loses it for my sake, shall gain it."

This self-denial is so complete that spiritual persons often mitigate it to justify conducting themselves upon this road in a very different way. They think that any kind of retirement and reformation of life will do it. They think that practicing the virtues, continuing in prayer and pursuing mortification is sufficient but they do not attain the spiritual purity that our Lord commends to us. Instead they prefer to feed and clothe their natural selves with spiritual feelings and consolations. They think it sufficient to deny themselves worldly things without annihilating and purifying themselves of spiritual desires. They flee from this solid and perfect spirituality that consists in the annihilation of all sweetness in God. They flee from aridity, distaste, and trial, which is the true spiritual cross and spiritual poverty in Christ. They seek only pleasurable communion with God. This is not self-denial and detachment of spirit but spiritual gluttony. Such a soul seeks itself in God rather than seeking God in itself. We must prefer nothing, absolutely nothing, to the love of

Christ. We must desire God for his own sake, and not for his gifts.

To seek one's self in God is to seek the gifts of God but to seek God in oneself is to be disposed to choose, for Christ's sake, all that is most distasteful, to endure afflictions, to go without consolation in relation to God and to the world. This is love of God. Our Lord greatly desires us to carry out this self-denial. It is like a death or annihilation, temporal, natural, and spiritual. One that saves one's life the same shall lose it.

When the two disciples asked Jesus for a place at his right hand, they wanted his gifts. He told them, rather, that they would drink the chalice that he would drink. This chalice symbolized his suffering and death. This is what the soul who loves God will choose, death to self. In this way it is not hindered, even by spiritual things, in taking the narrow way. The staff for this road is the cross by which the journey, contrary to all expectations, is made easy.

If the soul is resolved to meet trials and bear them for God's sake, it will find in them great relief and sweetness. In this way it can travel upon the road detached from all things and desiring nothing. If it should desire to possess anything, whether it comes from God or from any other source, with any sense of attachment, it has not denied itself and it will be unable to walk along this narrow path.

Spiritual persons should be aware that this road to God does not consist in multiplying meditations nor in consolations, however necessary these things may be to beginners; for this road the only thing that is needful is the ability to deny oneself sensually and spiritually, and give oneself up to suffering and total annihilation for the sake of Christ. As St. Paul says, "I live now, not I, but Christ lives in me." Unless the soul give itself to this annihilation, which is the sum and root of the virtues, it will profit not at all from all the other methods. Progress comes only through the imitation of Christ, who is the way, the truth, and the life. No one comes to the father but by him; he is the door. It seems then that any spirituality that would choose to walk in sweetness and with ease, and flee from the imitation of Christ, who carries the cross, is worthless.

When Christ said, "My God, my God, why have you forsaken me?," he accomplished the greatest work of his life, the salvation of mankind. But this was done at the moment when he was most completely annihilated, with respect to human reputation, spiritual and sensual consolation.

Those who consider themselves the friends of Christ often know him very little. They seek in him their own pleasures in consolations stemming from their self-love. Even worse, of course, are worldly persons, whether clerics aor not, eager about their own ambitions, reputations and wealth. They may be said not to know Christ at all, and their end will be very bitter.

Chapter 8

The Proximate Means of Divine Union

The proper and fitting means of union with God is faith. Nothing else, created or imagined, can serve the understanding as this proper means of union. Actually, anything that the understanding can attain, if it clings to it, is an impediment rather than a means to union.

It is a principle of philosophy that the means must be in proportion to the end. To choose a certain goal, the means we use must in some way be connected with and resemble that goal, at least enough for the desired end to be accomplished. So it is with our understanding. If it would be united with God in this life, so far as is possible, it must use that means that unites it with him and that bears the greatest resemblance to him. But no creature bears any resemblance to God's Being. All creatures have a certain relation to God and bear a divine impress, some more and others less, yet there is no essential resemblance or connection between them and God. On the contrary, the distance between their being and the Divine Being is infinite. As a result, it's impossible for the understanding to attain union with God by means of any creature, earthly or spiritual. There is no real resemblance between them. God is completely Other.

Everything that the understanding can receive in this life cannot be a proximate means of union with God. Nothing in nature can be a proximate means of union with God. So also, the forms and images of things in nature that are received through the senses into the mind cannot be the proximate means of union with God. In fact, the understanding in its bodily prison has no capacity for receiving the clear knowledge of God. This is why God told Moses that no man could see him and live. This is also why St. John tells us that no man has ever seen God.

If then the soul would be led directly to God, it must proceed by not understanding rather than desiring to understand, by not knowing rather than the desire to know. This is contemplation. It has the loftiest knowledge of God, called mystical theology, which signifies the secret wisdom of God. It is secret even to the understanding that receives it. This is why St. Denis calls it a ray of darkness, and a knowing of God that is not knowing. It is clear then that the understanding must be blind to all paths that are open to it in its natural capacity in order that it may be united to God. As a bat is blinded by the light of the sun, so is our understanding blinded by the light of God. This light becomes, as it were, total darkness to us. Furthermore, if the soul should seek to have its understanding use any created thing, natural or supernatural, to attain union with God, they would not only be a hindrance but even an occasion of many errors and delusions.

Chapter 9

Faith Is the Means to Divine Union

We have seen then that in order for the understanding to be prepared for Divine union, it must be void of all that pertains to sense, and freed from everything that can clearly be apprehended. The understanding must be put to silence and lean upon faith, which alone is the proximate means whereby the soul is united to God. Such is the likeness between faith and God, that there is no other difference between the two save that which exists between seeing God and believing in him. So, seeing God is essentially the same thing as faith in God. Faith is the substance of things that appear not. Faith, then, is the very substance of God. Even as God is infinite, faith sets him before us as infinite. Even as God is Three in One, faith sets him before us as Trinity. Faith can do what the intellect cannot do. The divine Light which passes all understanding manifests himself to the soul through faith. As the soul journeys to God, it must walk by faith with the understanding blinded and in darkness. This is a veritable cloud of unknowing within which God is hidden.

The obscurity of faith within which God is concealed is expressed in the Scriptures: "He made darkness, and the dark water, his hiding place." And "He set darkness under his feet." This points out the obscurity of faith wherein God is concealed. God appeared in darkness to Solomon in the Temple, and to Moses on the mountain. He spoke to Job from the darkness of the air. So it is clear that if the soul in this life wishes to attain to union with God and commune directly with him, it must unite itself with the darkness wherein God promised to dwell and where he is hidden. This is our faith.

CHAPTER 10

TYPES OF KNOWLEDGE

The soul may receive two ways of understanding, natural or supernatural. We have to understand these in order to direct the soul with greater clearness into the night of faith. The soul receives knowledge and intelligence naturally insofar as the understanding gets its intelligence through the bodily senses and what it does with the bodily senses by its own power. The soul receives knowledge and intelligence supernaturally when it is given to understand something over and above its natural ability. Normally we think of this as coming from God.

Supernatural knowledge can actually be physical in the sense that it comes from some supernaturally caused object known through the senses. This could be a vision of angels, extraordinary lights, or holy voices, etc. But supernatural knowledge can also be purely spiritual when the imagination is touched without any external physical stimulus. Thus a visionary can see the form of the Blessed Virgin but those around him see nothing. The vision is not there objectively, physically, externally, but only by means of the imagination being touched by God. This kind of knowledge is distinct in its nature but there is another kind of supernatural knowledge which is confused, general and dark. This kind of knowledge comes from contemplation which is given in faith. All the other kinds of knowledge are nothing but a means to this. They will lead to this only to the degree that we can actually detach ourselves from them.

Chapter 11

HINDRANCES

It seems strange to say but supernatural knowledge, which may very well come from God, can actually be a hindrance to the obscure or supernatural knowledge of contemplation that is the love of divine union and greatly to be desired. Can something that comes from God be a hindrance? Of course it can! In fact, everything comes from God, things that are helpful and things that hinder us. It depends on what we do with them, what our desire is and what our intention is.

We must mortify ourselves and be detached even from spiritual and supernatural understandings. We must reject them even if they come from God. This does not offend God and does not frustrate the reasons for which God gives us such knowledge. The very first moment that we receive supernatural knowledge from God, it produces its effect. From this point on, it must be rejected or it can be a hindrance to our contemplative love. The efficacy of such supernatural knowledge is not up to us, it is up to God. We must leave it in his hands. We must never rely upon it or even accept it but always fly from it. We should not even pause to ascertain whether such knowledge be good or evil.

If a supernatural vision is corporeal and exterior, it is probably not from God. Although we cannot limit what God can and may do. However, it is more proper and habitual for God to communicate himself in a totally spiritual way without involving the senses. When the senses are involved, there is always a great danger of deception by way of psychological aberrations, chemical imbalances, drugs, or alcohol. God does not need these things.

They are as different from the soul as the body is from the reasoning. Bodily sense is as ignorant of spiritual things as a beast is of rational things. Bodily sense makes its estimate of spiritual things by thinking that they are as it feels them to be, whereas they are very different. So that the soul that esteems such things errs greatly and is exposed to great danger of being deceived. Such a soul will also have within itself an impediment to the attainment of true spirituality because there is no proportion between spiritual things and bodily things. It is much safer to assume that such things come from the world, the flesh or the devil than from God.

The 21st century is replete with examples of how such things lead people into error and downright foolish activity. In the world today, there are dozens of pseudo-visionaries declaring to all and sundry messages supposedly given by corporeal visions of the Blessed Virgin. They can do much harm, sometimes even advocating activity contrary to the

teachings of the church, sometimes being directed unabash-
edly toward deceiving people for money. These are not from
God. People who run to such things are usually gullible and
lacking in the supernatural virtue of faith. The Scriptures,
Christ, and the teachings of the church are not enough for
them but they must run hither and yon titillating their curi-
osity, disobeying legitimate authority and causing great
harm to themselves and others.

Corporeal visions can communicate to a certain degree
some spirituality, as is always the case when they come from
God. However, much less is communicated by them than
would be the case if the same things were more interior and
spiritual. Since they are so palpable and material, they stir
the senses greatly and it appears to the judgment of the soul
that they are of greater importance because they are more
readily felt. Thus the soul goes after them readily, abandon-
ing faith and thinking that the light it receives from them is
the means to its desired goal, which is union with God. In
fact, the more attention the soul pays to such things, the
further it strays from that union. (Visions that are of God
penetrate the soul and move the will to love, and produce
their effect, which the soul cannot resist even if it wanted to.)

It is necessary for the spiritual person to deny him- or
herself all the understandings and the temporal delights that
belong to the outward senses. Otherwise he or she is in danger of falling further and further away from God. His or her
faith grows gradually less. He or she is spiritually hindered
because his or her soul rests in them rather than soaring to
the invisible. The soul becomes attached to these things and

does not advance to detachment. The soul sets its eyes on this sensual aspect, the least important, and begins to lose the effect of any inward spirituality that they might offer. The soul begins to accept God's favors as though they belonged to it and hence it does not profit by them as it should. They open the door to easy deception from the world, the flesh, and the devil. Thus it is always best for the soul to reject these things no matter where they may come from.

Let me conclude the subject by stating that the soul must be very careful never to accept these corporeal visions, save occasionally on the advice of an intelligent, mature, spiritual person. Even then the soul must have no desire for them.

CHAPTER 12

VISIONS THAT COME THROUGH THE IMAGINATION

Sometimes God touches our imagination and causes us a visionary experience in that interior sense. Here also it is impossible for the soul to attain union with God through such things. The imagination uses bodily figures and images. This can happen in two ways. One way is supernatural. In this way the representation is made passively without any effort of our own. The other way is natural. This is done by the natural ability of our souls, which use forms, figures and images.

Meditation, or mental prayer, comes about through this means. It is a discursive action that we bring about by means of images, forms and figures that are fashioned by our five senses. For example, when we imagine Christ crucified, or God seated upon the throne in majesty, or Jesus' Sermon on the Mount and all kinds of other things, whether Divine or human.

In order to enter into the dark night of the spirit, all these imaginings must be cast out. This kind of prayer, which is usually called discursive prayer, does not have a place here in the contemplation of divine Union. Of itself it is not a proximate means of union with God. The reason for this is that the imagination cannot fashion anything beyond that which it has experienced through its exterior senses—namely, things we experience through our seeing, hearing, touching, etc. None of these created things have any real resemblance to the Being of God and so they cannot serve as proximate means to union with God.

Certainly, for beginners it is necessary that we use our imagination in discursive prayer to enkindle our souls with love by means of the senses. Thus they do serve as a remote means to union with God. However, as the soul advances, it passes beyond this remote means and enters the dark night of faith in which the imagination has no place. It may be that the soul, even the advanced soul, may occasionally pray through discursive meditation but it does not play as important a role in the prayer or spirituality of this soul. The soul who wishes to enter into the contemplative dimension at any given time must abandon this kind of discursive meditation. St. Paul tells us in the Acts of the Apostles that we should never think of the Godhead by likening him to gold or to

silver, neither to stone that is formed by art, nor to anything
that humans can fashion by their imagination.

It is fitting that God leads beginners on to further spiritual blessings that are interior and invisible, by taking away
from them the pleasure of discursive meditation. These
beginners do not know how to detach themselves from the
sensible methods of prayer to which they have grown accustomed. They labor to retain them, desiring to proceed as customary by way of meditation upon forms, ideas and images,
not realizing that they must go beyond them. It is at this
point that the *Cloud of Unknowing* tells such souls to bury
all of their thoughts, images and ideas beneath the cloud of
forgetting.

When they do reach that point in their spiritual journey
where they are called to go beyond these things, they will
find that clinging to them simply causes aridity and weariness and disquiet of soul. If, when this happens, they consult
a spiritual director who is not him- or herself a contemplative, they can be greatly hindered in their journey to union
with God.

Souls that are no longer spiritual beginners, who should
have passed beyond the discursive meditation stage, sometimes find themselves dealing with this aridity and affliction because they are being held back by personal ignorance
or poor spiritual direction. They may actually have entered
into the contemplative dimension of union with God but do
not realize it. They think they are being idle, doing nothing, even sleeping. They do not allow themselves to remain
in repose but struggle to engage in forms of prayer that are

no longer befitting for them. They are trying to retrace the ground they have already traversed, and to seek to do that which has already been done.

They must be instructed to abide attentively and wait lovingly upon God in that state of quiet and pay no attention to the imagination and its images. It is time to allow God to work in them by his grace and in the darkness of faith. They must let go of all methods and manners and workings of the imagination. God will initiate the work of love. No one else can do this. It is to be noted, however, that once God does begin this work of love, it can be facilitated by spiritual teachings, some of which we will see later.

CHAPTER 13

SPIRITUAL SIGNS

There are certain signs that the spiritual soul will find in itself and through which it will know when it is right and proper for it to leave behind discursive meditation and pass to the state of contemplation. It is important that the soul should not lay aside this kind of prayer before the Spirit bids it nor hold onto it longer than is proper. There are three such signs. All three of them must be present. It is not sufficient that one or two of the signs are present because that can just be the normal dryness and challenges of prayer for the beginner. All three of these signs must be present.

This is the first sign. The soul realizes that he no longer takes pleasure in the methods of prayer he has been using. Rather it finds using its reason and imagination in mental prayer difficult and dry. If, perchance, the soul still finds pleasure in its discursive meditation and is able to reason, it should not abandon it, save when its soul is led into that peace and quiet which we will describe under the third sign.

The second sign is that the soul realizes it no longer desires to fix its mind or its senses upon particular objects, either interior or exterior. Its imagination will still come and go, which it will do even in times of deep recollection. But the soul will have no pleasure in fixing it, of set purpose, upon objects.

The third and most important sign is that the soul takes pleasure in being alone and, without making any particular meditation, waits with loving attentiveness upon God. The soul experiences an inward peace and rest without exercising its faculties of memory or understanding. The soul is alone with a general, obscure knowledge and loving without any particular understanding. This is a state of repose and rest in the presence of God but in darkness without the light of the intellect. St. Bernard even calls it a form of sleeping but it is, in fact, an attentiveness to the presence of God beyond imagination, words or ideas. Sometimes spiritual persons, with little knowledge of the spiritual journey and inadequate direction, will even erroneously think they actually have fallen asleep. But if all these three signs are present, let them understand that they have entered into the contemplative dimension of prayer.

When this contemplative experience first begins, the soul is hardly aware of this loving knowledge, which is apt, at this time, to be very subtle and almost imperceptible. The soul has been accustomed to discursive meditation that is completely perceptible and does not understand what is happening. It may even strive to restore its former way of mental prayer.

As the soul becomes more accustomed to contemplation, it will become more and more conscious of this loving general knowledge of God and its resultant peace without strenuous labor. This matter will be treated in greater detail in the first chapters of "The Dark Night of the Senses."

Chapter 14

The Fitness of these Signs

With respect to the first sign, the spiritual person desiring to enter upon the spiritual road of contemplation must leave behind the way of imagination and of meditation through the senses. He or she will only do this when he or she takes no more pleasure in them and is unable to focus on his or her ability to reason. This soul has already received those spiritual goods necessary to lead it up this road toward union with God. It finds no pleasure in this now because it has progressed as far as this level of prayer can lead it. It may not completely abandon discursive prayer, but it will have a lesser role than before. This advancing soul, at this point, by habitual practice possesses now the substance in the habit of the spirit of meditation. This is essentially the gaining of some knowledge and love of God. Each time the soul profits from this kind of meditation more and more and eventually it forms a habit. All of these many acts of loving knowledge that the soul has been making become habitual. At this point God will bring about in them this loving knowledge without the intervention of these acts, or at least, without as many of them. He will often set them at once in contemplation. The soul, which was gaining gradually through its labor of meditation upon particular facts, has now through habit become converted and changed. It now has a habit of loving knowledge, not as distinct and particular as it was before, but of an obscure, general kind.

St. Teresa tells us that our growth in prayer can be compared to the ways of drawing water for a garden. Instead of using buckets put down in a well or a waterwheel or even irrigation aqueducts, the water is now brought to the soul so that it drinks peacefully without labor. The soul now drinks of wisdom, love and delight albeit in an obscure, loving and passive way.

Unfortunately, many souls are led to believe that they must engage in the labor of continuous reasoning to understand particular things by means of images and forms. When they do not find this in their contemplative experience, they think they are going astray and wasting time. On the contrary, the less they perceive ideas and images, the further they penetrate into the night of the spirit through which they must pass in order to be united with God in a union transcending all knowledge. With respect to the second sign, it should be clear that the soul can no longer take pleasure in different sensible objects of the imagination. It is closer to God than to worldly things and so it will take pleasure only in God. The soul must remember, however, that the imaginative faculty, even in the state of recollection, is in the habit of coming and going of its own accord. The soul will be troubled by this because its peace and joy are disturbed.

It is here that many of the great mystics suggest that the soul should sum up all its desire for God in a prayer word. Walter Hilton suggests as a prayer word the name Jesus. The Cloud of Unknowing suggests a simple one syllable word such as "God" or "love." This prayer word will serve as an aid to help the soul to bury all this activity of the imagination beneath the cloud of forgetting. The word is gently repeated as often as necessary to help the soul focus on this obscure, loving knowledge of God rather than on the images of the imagination.

The third sign is a peaceful, loving attentiveness or obscure knowledge of God. This comes when discursive reasoning and imaginative images cease. If the soul did not, at this time, have this knowledge of God and this realization of his presence, it would do nothing and have nothing. (This would be to fall into, what has been called, the heresy of Quietism). Instead the soul has, at this time, an obscure knowledge of God, in this night of spirit, with a loving faith-filled realization of his presence. The soul exercises its spiritual faculties; namely, the memory, the understanding and the will. By means of these spiritual faculties, the soul has a graced fruition of the sensible faculties even though the sensible faculties have no part to play in the experience.

Because of this the soul seems to be in darkness when it is really basking in the light of God. At times, the soul does not perceive darkness or light nor apprehend anything that it knows from any source whatsoever. It seems to remain in a great forgetfulness so that, temporarily, it does not know where it has been or what it has done or even of the passage of time. When the soul does return to itself, after a greater or lesser period of time, it believes that less than a moment has passed, or no time at all. In the contemplative experience, the soul goes beyond any consciousness of time.

It might be helpful, at this point, to see how some mystics other than John of the Cross deal with this subject. One very prominent teacher of the contemplative experience is Guigo II, a Carthusian monk of the 12th century. He wrote what is called "The Ladder For Monks." He tells us that prayer is like a ladder planted firmly in the earth with four rungs leading up into the heavens. As we climb this ladder, we enter step-by-step into divine union with God in contemplative prayer.

The first rung of the ladder is Lectio Divina. This means spiritual reading. It can be any kind of spiritual reading but primarily the Scriptures. The second rung of the ladder is meditation (meditatio). This refers to discursive or mental prayer. So we advance from the first rung by meditating on the Scripture reading. The third rung is oratio or prayer. This is a special kind of prayer sometimes called affective prayer. It is a prayer that results from the meditation on the Scripture reading that fills the heart with love. It has a certain kind of élan or spiritual fervor. It is usually a brief prayer, the kind that "pierces the heavens." This prayer is often shortened to one or two words summing up the desire for God that is in the heart. The fourth rung of the ladder is contemplation. The soul is led into contemplation by this brief prayer.

Very often this "Ladder" of Guigo II is referred to simply as Lectio Divina, subsuming all of the steps into the first one. A good example of that is found in William of St. Thierry, a 13th century Cistercian monk, in his letter to the Carthusians, sometimes called "The Golden Epistle." He says that fixed hours, specified times, should be given to Lectio Divina. It should not be haphazard reading as if lighted on simply by chance. This does not edify but makes the mind unstable. Taken lightly into the memory it goes out from it even more lightly. It is better to choose the Scriptures or specific authors and concentrate on them.

The Scriptures especially need to be read in the same spirit in which they were written. To understand St. Paul's meaning, the soul must apply itself constantly to reading him and meditating on him. The same is true with the psalms. You must make the sentiments of the psalms your own through frequent and consistent meditation. There is the same gulf between attentive study and mere reading as there is between friendship and acquaintance.

Some small part of your daily reading should also be committed each day to memory. It should be taken, as it were, into the stomach, to be more carefully digested and brought up again for frequent rumination. This memory passage should be in keeping with your vocation and helpful for your concentration. It should be something that will take hold of your mind and save it from distraction. It may be something as small as just a word or two.

The reading should also stimulate your feelings and give rise to affective prayer. Whenever this happens, you should allow it to interrupt your reading. It does not so much interfere with the reading as it restores to it a mind evermore purified for understanding. If the soul truly seeks God in its reading, everything it reads will tend to promote its purpose or intention, which is to make the mind surrender to God and bring all that it understands into Christ's service in love.

Another mystic who teaches us about contemplative prayer is St. Bernard of Clairvaux. Rather than give us a method, as such, St. Bernard describes the experience of contemplation. In his Sermon 52, St. Bernard speaks of the contemplative experience as repose or sleep. It is a special sleep that is given by the Lord to those whom he loves as a bridegroom loves his bride. This sleep of the bride is not the tranquil repose of the body that, for a while, sweetly lulls the fleshly senses. It is a slumber that is vital and watchful, which enlightens the heart, drives away death, and communicates eternal life. It is a genuine sleep yet it does not stupefy the mind but transports it.

Another mystic is Walter Hilton, an Augustinian from 14th century England. In his great work, "The Ladder of Success," he speaks of the three parts of contemplative prayer. In chapter 3, he says, "Contemplative life consists in perfect love, felt inwardly by spiritual values; and in a true and certain sight and knowledge of God and spiritual matters. This life belongs especially to those who, for the love of God, forsake all worldly riches, honors, and outward businesses and wholly give themselves, soul and body, (insofar as they can) to the service of God by exercises of the soul."

Walter Hilton says that contemplative life has three parts. The first part consists in knowing God and spiritual things through our natural reasoning, by the teaching of humans, and the study of holy Scripture. This is done, however, without spiritual affection or inward relish being felt; in other words, without affection. They do not have that special gift of the Holy Spirit that is had by persons truly spiritual in their understanding. These are learned persons, who through long study in theology and Scripture, attain knowledge to their natural ability. This is something given to every person who has the use of reason. This knowledge is good and may be considered a part of contemplation as it is a study of truth and a knowledge of spiritual things. It is, however, but a figure or shadow of true contemplation since it has no spiritual affection in God that is felt by only one who has a great love of God. St. Paul spoke of this when he said, "If I knew all mysteries and all knowledge, but did not have charity, I am nothing."

This knowledge could lead to true contemplation if possessed in humility and charity but it could also become puffed up with pride and lead to the desire for worldly honors. Again St. Paul says, "Knowledge puffs up, but charity edifies." Through prayer the Lord will turn this cold and unsavory knowledge into true wisdom as he turned the water into wine.

The second part of contemplation lies principally in affection but without spiritual light in the understanding. This is usually found in simple and unlearned persons who give themselves to devotion. They will practice mental prayer and, through the grace of the Holy Spirit, will feel the fervor of love and spiritual sweetness. They will also experience a certain reverential fear towards God. In prayer they find the powers of their soul gathered together in the love of their hearts drawn up from all transitory things, aspiring toward God by a fervent desire. During this time they have no specific understanding of particular spiritual things but only a kind of obscure knowledge. They take delight in this kind of prayer and out of it may come tears of joy, burning desires for God and contrition for sin. Thus their hearts are cleansed from all sin and melts into a wonderful sweetness in Jesus. They become obedient and ready to fulfill God's will without reckoning what may become of themselves. These feelings come only with a special grace. This fervor does not always come at will, nor last a long time. It comes and goes as God wills.

There is a higher degree to the second sort of contemplation that is had by those who are in great rest and quiet of both body and mind. By the grace of Jesus and by long travail, physical and spiritual, they arrive to a rest and quietness of heart. It pleases them greatly to be still and to think on the Lord and the name of Jesus. For them all other kinds of prayers, such as the Our Father or the Hail Mary, are turned into a spiritual joy.

There is a third part of contemplation, according to Walter Hilton, which is perfect, insofar as that can be had in this life. It consists in knowing and loving God by a soul reformed into the image of Jesus by the perfection of virtues. The person is taken from all earthly affection, from vain thoughts, from images of all bodily creatures and taken up from his or her bodily senses and enlightened by the Holy Spirit to see truth itself. He or she becomes ravished with God's love and conformed to the image of the Trinity. This perfect contemplation may be begun in this life but its full perfection is reserved for the bliss of heaven.

Another great mystical work of the 14th century, the anonymous "Cloud of Unknowing," speaks of the necessity for beginners of the first three rungs of Guigo's ladder for monks. He then goes on to speak of the fourth rung, contemplative prayer, which, he says, is his only concern. In chapter 3, he says, "This is what you are to do. Lift your heart up to the Lord with a gentle stirring of love, desiring him for his own sake and not for his gifts." In chapter 7 he says, "If you wish, you may express that desire in a simple word of one syllable such as 'God' or 'love.'" He tells us to use this word, when our imagination and intellect would distract us by words and images, to beat upon the cloud of unknowing above us. Walter Hilton and Jan Ruysbroek (a 14th-century Flemish mystic) suggest that we use the name of Jesus as our prayer word.

He also tells us that a person, if he or she would be a contemplative, must destroy the radical, self-centered awareness of his or her own being. In doing this, every possible obstacle to divine union would be destroyed. This is done by the realization of his or her nothingness (humility) which will lead him or her into an awareness of the everyness of God. In order to do this, a person must empty him- or herself of everything sensible and spiritual. A person no longer cares about him- or herself, if only he or she can love God.

It should be clear that all of these mystics are saying the same thing that John of the Cross says but each with his own nuance. John of the Cross, however, speaks with the repetitiousness and thoroughness of a good teacher.

Let us return to the "Ascent of Mount Carmel." On the contemplative level, the soul remains as though ignorant of all things, for it knows God only without knowing how. This is referred to as an obscure knowledge or, sometimes, as the knowledge of love. In the state of knowledge the soul believes itself to be doing nothing, and to be entirely unoccupied, because it is working neither with the senses nor with the interior faculties.

The "Cloud of Unknowing" warns beginners that it is not unusual to feel nothing but a kind of darkness about the mind: "The soul will seem to know nothing and feel nothing except a naked intent toward God in the depths of his being."

John of the Cross assures the soul that it is not wasting time. Sometimes this knowledge is called a general kind of knowledge. It does not focus on anything in particular but it is aware that it is loving God. If the soul discerns within itself the three signs previously mentioned, even though it seems to be doing nothing, it will be well occupied.

CHAPTER 15

FOR CONTEMPLATIVE BEGINNERS

Those who have experienced the beginnings of contemplation should not think that they may never go back to their previous forms of praying, especially mental prayer. They should occasionally meditate and reason in their accustomed natural way. When they observe in their contemplative experience that the soul is not, at any given time, occupied in that repose and obscure knowledge we have spoken of, they will need to make use of mental prayer. This will be true until they become proficients and acquire, in some degree, the perfection of the habit of contemplation. Then if they begin mental prayer, they will experience that they no longer desire to do so because the knowledge and peace of divine union will be given them.

Such a soul will frequently find itself in this loving or peaceful state of waiting upon God while in no way exercising its own faculties in respect to particular acts. As we have said, in order to reach this state, it will frequently need to make use of discursive meditation quietly and in moderation. Then the soul waits upon God, loving him for his own sake and not for his gifts. Until the soul reaches this stage, that of the proficient, it will sometimes use the one and sometimes the other kind of meditation as needed. In contemplative prayer, we say that the soul does not work at all. It does not understand in its usual way. It understands things without taxing its own industry and receives only that which is given to it by God. The knowledge of God in the state will be general and obscure but this is necessary to receive this divine light more abundantly. Former ways of understanding, which may be more palpable, are so unlike even this obscure knowledge of God that they would interfere with it.

When the spiritual person cannot engage in discursive meditation, let him or her learn to be still in God and fix his or her loving attention upon Him. Although the spiritual person may think him- or herself to be doing nothing, little by little, divine calm and peace will be infused in his or her soul. He or she will have a wondrous and sublime, albeit obscure, knowledge of God. As the psalm tells us, "Be still and know that I am God."

CHAPTER 16

THE IMAGINATION

The imagination can work in two ways. It can work naturally by taking forms and images given through the imagination and reproducing them in the mind in a natural way. It can also do this in an imaginative way; that is, by making these images more unusual, extraordinary and even more beautiful than they were seen by the actual senses. But the imagination can also be touched supernaturally so that it can use images from the senses at the disposal of God or even from the devil.

No one can limit the activity of God or determine the divine will. But, it must be said that, ordinarily, God does not use the imagination to communicate supernatural things. This is not true of the devil, the world or the flesh. By that I mean that the imagination can be touched in ways that are or seem supernatural by evil influences, such as the devil, drugs, or even psychological aberrations. Because of this it is strongly advisable that we reject all such visions in the dimension of our imagination decisively and immediately.

But, you may say, does this not put us in danger of rejecting a vision in the imagination which is from God. Not at all. If God should give the soul such a vision, it will produce its effect by God's will and not by ours. Once it is given, it will be effective and we are justified by taking the safer course that is simply to reject it, knowing that God has already brought about the results that he wanted. There is really no human way of telling whether such a vision comes from God, from the devil, from drugs or from psychological deviations. So we reject them all and place it in God's hands. Any divine communication is, after all, as God wills. This is told to you simply to instruct the soul that it may not be hindered or impaired as to union with Divine Wisdom through good visions, nor deceived by those which are false.

Such visions, whether from God or from the devil, must not be desired, nor, if given, should we cling to them. This would, indeed, be a form of attachment and hinder our journey to divine union. We must remember that God does not come within any individual image nor is he contained within any particular kind of idea. In this life, God is hidden in darkness, in a cloud of unknowing. No form or figure that is possible in this life can bring the soul to union with God.

Faith is the true medium that leads the soul to God. And faith is the substance of things which appear not. It is not found in visions, natural or supernatural. Sincere and simple souls have safe and sound teaching from the Church, which is that of faith. St. Peter had a vision of glory in which he saw Christ at the Transfiguration yet in his second Epistle he tells us that this vision should not be taken for an important and sure testimony. He directed his readers to faith, telling them we have a sure testimony in the words of the prophets who bear witness to Christ. Cling only to that dark light which is faith.

CHAPTER 17

THROUGH THE SENSES

In the Book of Wisdom, we are told that God orders all things with sweetness. Theologians tell us that God moves all things according to their nature. This is why God leads the soul onward by instructing it through forms and images from the senses. He does this naturally and supernaturally according to the soul's method of understanding. This is how the two extremes, the human and the Divine, sense and spirit, are brought to union. God brings a person to perfection according to the way of a person's own nature. He works from what is lowest and most exterior to what is highest and most interior. First he perfects the bodily senses leading the person by way of them to make use of good things. Then with this preparation, he perfects them still further by giving them certain supernatural favors and gifts. This may be through visions of holy things or Saints in corporeal shape, through spiritual speaking or other imaginary, supernatural graces. Thus he goes from the lower to the higher, which is the natural order and God's ordinary method. It must be understood, however, that God is totally free to cause the soul to advance in any way that he wishes. It is not necessary for him to observe this, or any other order.

So in the beginning God gradually leads the soul to himself by the senses. We delight in seeing holy and beautiful things, in tasting and realizing that the Lord is good, in hearing holy and edifying words, in pious meditations, in seeing God in his creation. Then he may take us a further step and use these sensible things to give us supernatural visions based on them. But then God leads us through these ways of the flesh beyond the ways of the flesh. These things lose their savors. They become insipid. There is a kind of emptiness that amounts to a yearning for God who alone can fill it. It cannot be filled by anything less than God and we are gradually led to this desire and this realization.

There is a temptation to cling to these sensual things because we are used to them and they are all that we have ever known. This is where the dark night of the senses comes in. We have to be led away from them, whether they be natural or supernatural (but based on the senses).

We must be cautious in regard to supernatural things given to us in the manner of the senses. This would include locutions (voices), visions of angels or saints, or any spiritual thing communicated through sensual images. There is always a danger of clinging to them for their own sake, for self-satisfaction or even through a prideful motivation. This is why they must be rejected immediately. This is not offensive to God because he will bring about the graces he wants them to communicate without any effort on our part. By rejecting these things, the soul does not hinder the blessings that God wishes to communicate through them.

By doing this the soul frees itself from the dangers and the efforts inherent in trying to decide between evil visions and good ones. Such visions can come from God, from the devil, from the world or from the flesh (drugs or unhealthy psyches). Sometimes there is just no way to know. So they are all to be rejected and the soul must trust in God without the use of such things. The soul must focus upon the spiritual good these things may produce in its actions for the service of God. If we should be told or inspired in a vision to do something that is clearly loving and compatible with our service of God, we should do it. Otherwise everything should be ignored. Nothing contrary to the spirit of devotion and love of God should be received from such visions. The visions themselves must not be clung to. God does not give them for their own sake but only to lead us to himself.

◆

Chapter 18

Further Admonitions

There is a danger of being over-credulous regarding visions, even if they be of God. Certain spiritual directors show a lack of discretion in this regard. They may embarrass or mislead the client by speaking highly of their visions and making an overly great account of them. When the soul sees in its confessor esteem for visions of the senses, it will become attached to them and pridefully value them over the darkness of faith which alone can lead to divine union. If the spiritual father has an attraction toward revelations of such a kind, so will the soul in his care. The director may even beg to the soul to pray to God to reveal such visions to themselves. They then take a natural pleasure in them and frequently go astray. They blindly trust these revelations and their own interpretation of them.

Chapter 19

Deceptions

Even if visions and interior locutions (spiritual words) come from God, we may be deceived about them. Coming from God, they are always true and certain in themselves. With respect to ourselves, however, we may understand them in a defective manner. We may also be deceived by way of the manner in which God sends them. When God promised Abraham the land of the Canaanites, Abraham misunderstood. God had finally to clarify this by telling him it would be given not to Abraham himself but to his off-spring after a period of 400 years. If Abraham had acted according to his own understanding of God's promise, he would have been greatly deceived. So it is that souls are often deceived with respect to revelations that come from God because they misinterpret them according to their own limited understanding. The darkness of faith must still be taken into consideration. The language of God is very different from ours. It is a spiritual language and very far removed from our understanding. Many times in the Old Testament God's people understood revelations literally. They took them to refer to events that were occurring in their own day. The Holy Spirit, however, has shown us that these revelations were not prophecies in the literal sense. In fact, they referred to the coming of the Messiah, still several hundred years in the future.

Even prophecies concerning Christ had to be understood spiritually, as he explained to Pilate when he told him that his kingdom was not of this world. His very own disciples misunderstood the prophecies and even the words of Christ as referring to a temporal kingdom. Thus it is clear that although revelations may be from God, we cannot always be sure of their meaning. We can easily be deceived because of our manner of understanding them. The spiritual director should therefore be careful that the soul under his or her care be not led astray to the extent that he or she retains no spiritual truth at all from God's revelations. Indeed, he or she must wean the soul from every sort of vision or locution and impress upon him or her the need of remaining in the freedom and darkness of faith. Also he or she must teach his or her client that the meaning of God's revelation is always spiritual and elevated in preference to temporal and mundane.

CHAPTER 20

REVELATIONS ARE TRUE BUT NOT ALWAYS STABLE

God's revelations are always true but not always stable in relation to ourselves. God often makes statements founded upon creatures and their effects that are changeable and liable to fail. In the Old Testament God revealed that the city of Nineveh would be destroyed in 40 days. This did not happen because the cause of the threat, the sins of the city, were repented of. So we see here that God's revelation was founded upon changeable creatures and their effects. The threat revealed by God was true but it was dependent upon the subsequent response of the people of Nineveh. So we see that, although God may have revealed something to a soul, this may be changed or altered depending upon some change made by the soul. God's revelation was bound up with human causes that may thus render the revelation no longer relevant. The individual soul cannot understand the hidden truths of God that are in his revelations. God speaks according to the way of eternity, while we blind souls understand only the ways of flesh. Let us understand that God's ways are not to be questioned. He will bring us in his own time and in his own way to a complete understanding.

<h2>Chapter 21</h2>

<h2>Supernatural Methods</h2>

At times God will answer prayers that seek extraordinary, supernatural responses. Because he answers them, the souls think that it is a good method and pleasing to God. It is not a good method. God has laid down rational and natural limits in his dealings with humans. It is not lawful to desire to pass beyond them by supernatural means, nor is it pleasing to God. You may say then why does God answer such requests? It isn't always God who answers; sometimes it's the devil. If it is God who answers, he does so because of the weakness of the soul. God is like a spring from which everyone draws water according to the vessel that he or she carries. Some good souls may be very weak and God answers them according to that weakness. But it is his wish that actually they be stronger and not need these methods. When the Israelites asked God to give them a king, he gave them one. He did so unwillingly because it was not good for them. They, however, would not or could not proceed by any other road because of their weakness and so he granted it to them.

It is not good to desire to know things by supernatural means. It is even worse to desire spiritual favors pertaining to the senses. The soul has its natural reason and the doctrine and law of the Gospel, which are quite sufficient for its guidance. There is no problem that cannot be remedied by these means. This is very pleasing to God and of great profit to souls. Human reasoning, together with the teachings of the Gospel, should be sufficient for us. If we should receive certain things supernaturally, whether at our request or not, we must receive only that which is in clear conformity with reason and Gospel law. We should receive it not because it is revelation, but because it is reasonable. We must beware deceptions from the devil in this area. When a soul is in need and experiencing trials and difficulties, there is no better means than prayer and the hope that God will provide for us according to his will. Error and confusion usually fall to those who desire special, supernatural methods from God to solve their problems. The world, the flesh and the devil are great imitators of God and can easily deceive us. They are like the wolf in sheep's clothing. They can even use the truth to deceive us. They do not have power over supernatural means but they can use natural means with such acuity that they can deceive us into believing that it is supernatural. God is not pleased when we dispose ourselves to be deceived by these means by praying or expecting special, supernatural interventions. Anyone who has eyes to see and ears to hear will recognize the folly of apparently spiritual persons who lose themselves in such deceits. Is it any wonder why God can be said to be angry at such kind of prayers? People who make them cannot be satisfied with faith. They do not see faith as the light of God's revelation but as a kind of debilitating darkness.

Chapter 22

Praying for a Miracle?

We have seen now, in the previous chapter, that souls should not desire to receive anything distinctly, by supernatural means, such as visions and locutions. This was permitted in the Old Testament and even commanded by God. We must understand, however, that it was permitted for prophets and priests to seek visions and revelations from God in the Old Testament because at that time faith did not have the firm foundation given to us in the New Testament. Also now we have the law of the Gospel in which God speaks to us in the fullness of his revelation in Christ. Our faith is founded in Christ, and in this time of grace, the law of the Gospel has been made manifest. We do not need further revelation. We have the Holy Spirit who reminds us of everything that Jesus taught. If we have the faith of a grain of mustard seed, all our needs, trials and temptations can be resolved through Christ and the Gospels as the Holy Spirit gives them to us. God has spoken through Christ once and for all in this single Word. He has no occasion to speak further. St. Paul tells us that in the past God spoke in sundry ways and in diverse manners. But now, in these last days, he has spoken to us once and for all in his Son. What need have we now of special supernatural visions and revelations?

It may be that if we are weak in our faith, and so pray, God will answer our prayers but he cannot be really pleased with such prayers when they come in the face of what he has already revealed in Christ. The faith we are given in our baptism, and which is renewed in the sacraments, is sufficient for us. Nothing to be found in locutions, visions, or spiritual personal revelations cannot be found through our normal Christian faith.

Are you asking for Christ again as though he were never given? Were his teachings in vain? His death and resurrection without value? His sending of the Holy Spirit useless? Is it any wonder that the Father is not pleased with our asking for further revelations? He may give them, on a personal level, because of weakness of faith but the dangers of such an experience are very great. Deception is almost inevitable as we have seen.

Do you need a word of consolation? Look at Christ and see how fully he answers you. Do you want to understand the deep mysteries of faith? Set your eyes on Christ and the wisdom and wondrous things of God that are hidden in him will be revealed. Does not St. Paul tell us that in the Son of God are hidden all the treasures of wisdom and the knowledge of God? In Christ dwells all the fullness of the Godhead bodily. It is neither fitting nor necessary that we should ask for more. To ask for more is to find fault with God for not having given us a sufficiency in Christ.

When Christ said on the cross "It is finished," he indicated that his human ministry was complete and that the world had been given all that the Father desired to bring about its salvation. So by reason of the law of Christ, the teaching of the Gospel and the ministry of the church, we are able, in a human and visible manner, to remedy all our spiritual weaknesses and ignorance. If anyone, even an angel, should teach us anything else, he or she is accursed, St. Paul warns us.

In the Old Testament God spoke to his people through priests and prophets. In the New Testament, we are all priests and prophets. God is present where there are two of us gathered together in his name. He speaks to us, not where there is one alone, but in the church, which is the body of Christ. He speaks to us now and confirms us in our weakness, and our trials, through the ministers of the church who can make clear and confirm the truth in our hearts. Qualified and approved spiritual directors are the ministers of the church, as well as qualified superiors. Without them the soul can be weak and feeble in the truth, but together with them, it can be strong in the face of the world, the flesh and the devil. Remember how St. Paul tells us that he heard the Gospel, not from man but from God. Yet he could not be satisfied until he had consulted with St. Peter and the apostles lest perhaps he should run in vain. Anything revealed by God to an individual should be brought to the church—that is, to a competent member of the body of Christ—for confirmation. For a soul to consult only with itself means that it is its own spiritual director. Such a one, says St. Bernard of Clairvaux, has a fool for a director!

We must point out that, even though we have insisted that extraordinary revelations should be set aside, confessors should not show displeasure in regard to them. They must not make their penitents hesitant or afraid to mention them. In view of the difficulty that some souls experience in talking about such matters and the need for consultation, they should be encouraged, in a kindly and patient manner, to speak of them.

CHAPTER 23

SPIRITUAL APPREHENSIONS

Up until now, I have been speaking of revelations, visions, and locutions, etc., which come to the understanding through the senses. This may be either directly through these five senses or indirectly through the senses by way of the imagination. I refer to them as apprehensions of the understanding that come by means of sense. My intention was to disencumber the understanding of them and direct the soul into the night of faith. Now I would like to treat of apprehensions of the understanding that come in a purely spiritual way.

There are four apprehensions of the understanding that are surely spiritual. Unlike the corporeal and imaginary communications, which come by way of the senses, these come without the intervention of any inward or outward corporeal sense. They present themselves to the understanding, clearly and distinctly, by supernatural and passive means. They come without the performance of any act on the part of the soul. These may be visions, revelations, locutions or spiritual feelings. Speaking in a general sense, all these four may be called visions of the soul. When the soul understands something, we say it sees them. So these four spiritual approaches to the intellect may be called *seeings* or spiritual visions. They are communicated to the soul directly by supernatural means and not through sensible means.

Just as we did with the corporeal visions, leading the soul into the dark night of the senses, so also here we should disencumber the understanding from spiritual visions, leading the soul into the dark night of the spirit. This is faith leading to divine union.

The spiritual visions are nobler and more profitable and much more certain than sensible visions. They are interior and purely spiritual and are least able to be counterfeited by the world, the flesh and the devil. In spite of that the understanding may still be encumbered by them upon the road to divine union and, by its own imprudence, to be greatly deceived.

❧

Chapter 24

Two Kinds of Visions

Purely spiritual visions that can be received by the understanding may be about corporeal substances or incorporeal substances. The corporeal visions deal with material things of creation that the soul is given to see by a supernatural illumination. St. John, in the 21st chapter of the Book of Revelations, saw the heavenly Jerusalem. St. Benedict in a spiritual vision saw the whole world.

Incorporeal spiritual visions, such as angels, are not of this life nor can they be seen in the mortal body in essence as they are. These visions occur only occasionally and fleetingly in this life. When they happen, God totally withdraws the soul from this life. When St. Paul was drawn to the third heaven and saw things of which he could not speak, he was given this kind of vision. These are only given to those who are very strong in the faith. These visions are felt in the very substance of the soul.

Spiritual visions are much clearer and subtler than visions of the senses. They are like a flash of lightning on the dark night, revealing things suddenly, clearly and distinctly, and then leaving the soul in darkness. Yet what the soul sees in that light remains impressed upon it in a brilliantly clear way. They are never removed completely from the soul but, in time, they become somewhat remote.

The effects which these visions produce in the soul are illumination, quiet, joy, purity and love, humility and elevation of the spirit in God—sometimes one, sometimes the other, sometimes more, sometimes less. The world, the flesh and the devil can also produce these visions by aping them according to certain natural properties. St. Matthew tells us how the devil did this with Christ by showing him all the kingdoms of the world and the glory thereof. This vision, however, was not productive of humility and love of God, neither did it remain impressed upon the soul with sweetness and love.

Spiritual visions, inasmuch as they are of creatures, have no essential conformity with God and cannot serve the understanding as a proximate means of union with him. For this reason the soul must conduct itself in a negative way concerning them so that it might proceed to union of God by the proximate means of faith. So the soul must set no great store by them. The remembrance of them might lead the soul to a certain love of God in contemplation, yet the soul is exalted much more by pure faith and detachment in darkness. The more the soul desires obscurity with respect to all things, outward and inward, the more it is infused by faith and, consequently, by love and hope. God is incomprehensible and transcends all things so it is well for us to journey to him by denying ourselves of all things.

~

Chapter 25

Revelations

There are two kinds of revelation. The one is disclosure to the understanding of intellectual knowledge. The other is the manifestation of hidden mysteries of God.

Chapter 26

Very Spiritual Things

We speak now of spiritual visions that are very rare, experienced only by certain souls, and which can hardly be spoken of. We speak of them here briefly for completeness sake and as an aid to directors. We speak now of the intuition of naked truths in the understanding. The knowledge of naked truth is very different from what we have been speaking about. It consists in an understanding by the intellect of the truths of God. It can be about God or about creatures. When it is about God, it is impossible to compare it to anything else and there are no words to describe it. This is knowledge of God himself.

This is pure contemplation. It is about this experience that Marguerite Porete says, "No man can speak." The soul may speak of it in certain general terms of delight and felt blessing but that is all. Sometimes the Scriptures speak of this as something more to be desired than gold and very much more than precious stones and sweeter than the honey and the honeycomb. Actually, there are no words adequate to express this experience. St. Paul says that it is not lawful for a man to speak of it. It is beyond the power of the devil to meddle with such things or to produce anything that is like it. The soul cannot receive these touches by its own knowledge or imagination. It comes directly from God. These divine touches may come suddenly without any preparation or they may come by the mere recollection of certain things, even very small things. They may be strong or faint but they are always certain. The soul should not desire to have them, not desire not to have them, but must humbly accept them. The soul does not reject them as it does previous forms of revelations. It must be noted, however, that these favors are not granted to the soul which still cherishes attachments of any kind. They are presented to the soul through a very special love of God by way of great detachment.

These divine touches may also have reference to creatures. But they are given independently of any external suggestion and cannot come from deception. In some ways they are like the spirit of prophecy to which the soul gives a complete, passive, interior consent. It is a faith consent in which the soul journeys by believing rather than by understanding.

King Solomon gives us a marvelous statement of this experience when he says, "God has given me true knowledge of things that are: to know the disposition of the round world and the virtues of the elements; the beginning, and ending, and midst of the times, the alterations in the changes and the consummations of the seasons, and the changes of customs, the divisions of the seasons, the courses of the year and the disposition of the stars; the natures of animals, and the furies of the beasts, the strength and virtue of the winds, and the thoughts of man; the diversities in plants and trees and the virtues of roots and all things that are hidden, and those that are not foreseen: all these I learned, for Wisdom, which is the worker of all things, talks to me."

The soul must be very scrupulous in rejecting all kinds of revelations and seek to journey to God by the way of unknowing. It must be faithful in consulting its spiritual director and obedient to him or her. The director, for his or her part, to guide the soul, must lay no stress upon these things. They are not important vis-á-vis divine union. When these things are granted to the soul passively, they have their effect as God wills. This occurs without any necessity for the soul to exert any diligence in the matter and thus, on a practical scale, can simply ignore such interventions.

CHAPTER 27

HIDDEN MYSTERIES

A personal revelation may involve the revealing of hidden secrets or mysteries. They may be mysteries regarding God in himself, such as the most holy Trinity, or mysteries regarding God in his works. This would include the meaning of the Scriptures and the doctrines of the church and their application to real, historical events. We see such revelations in the Book of Revelations. Here we also see something of the myriad ways in which such revelations are given. God grants such things still in our time to whom he will. These are not new revelations but simply explanations of what has already been revealed in the Scripture and the teachings of the church. Error, misunderstandings and misinterpretations can easily occur. So anything that is revealed to us as new or different must not be consented to even if it was, as St. Paul warns us, spoken by an angel from heaven. To avoid deception, the soul must place its faith on the revelations of the Scripture and the doctrines of the church and not to anything which is revealed subsequent to them.

This is a very delicate matter. Spiritual souls should not desire to know things that are not revealed in the Scriptures or the teachings of the church. There are many instances in our day of private revelations, most of them not approved by the church, in which people run to learn more than their faith will tell them. This is really caused by a lack of true faith. They put their trust in some individual, sincere or deceived, to find out new, sensational things revealed—e.g., usually by the blessed Virgin. When they do not receive the support of the church, they will say that they are supported by the blessed Virgin Mary and her testimony is greater than that of the church. This alone should warn any intelligent person of the folly of such belief. What a festival this sort of thing provides for the world, the flesh and the devil.

❧

Chapter 28

Interior Locutions

W e will now speak of another kind of revelation, super-natural locutions. These may come to the spiritual soul without the intervention of any of the physical senses. When such a soul is inwardly recollected, certain clear and distinct words may be received. They may also come when the spirit is not recollected, not as formal words but, in some way, the essence or meaning of words is communicated.

Chapter 29

Words or Locutions in Recollection

W hen the soul is deep in meditation, the Holy Spirit can assist it in producing a series of reasonable and logical thoughts about the subject of its meditation so that the reasoning reveals things which the soul did not know previously. By its meditation, the soul is united with mysteri-ous truths of the faith. The Holy Spirit is also united with the soul in that truth. Thus aided by the Holy Spirit, the soul is able to reason to conclusions that reveal even further truths. This is one of the ways in which the Holy Spirit teaches. In this spiritual enlightenment of the understanding, no decep-tion is produced. However, on its own, the soul may con-tinue to reflect on these truths and fall into error. The reason for this is that the truths so revealed by the Holy Spirit are so subtle and spiritual that our reasoning, of its own accord, does not have a clear understanding of it. At such times it will seem to the soul as though a third person were speaking which the soul may attribute to God. Some souls may communicate such experiences to others as though they came from God. These communications can be false, misleading and even heretical. Their errors come from themselves but they think they come from God.

One can see that it is extremely important for souls to be humble and reveal all such spiritual experiences to their confessors. Such experiences should engender humility and charity as well as mortification and holy simplicity. If they do not do this, what is their value? It is true that the Holy Spirit might illuminate a recollected understanding. The greatest recollection, however, is done in faith. The purer the faith of the soul, the more it has of the infused charity of God. The more charity it has, the more it is illumined by the Holy Spirit. This illumination comes through faith and not through understanding and is far greater and more profound than any revelation communicated to the understanding. Revelations that require the application of the understanding can lead the soul astray. So we should not apply the understanding to things which are being supernaturally communicated. Rather we should simply and lovingly look to the will of God and passively receive it.

Let the soul learn to be intent upon nothing except grounding its will in humble love and imitating the Son of God in his life and mortifications. This is the road to union with God. So let us understand that various locutions may come to the understanding from the Holy Spirit, from natural illumination however subtle it may be, and from the devil who may speak to the soul by subtle suggestions.

The best sign that we can use for discernment in these situations is to apply the principle, "By their truths you shall know them." When the soul finds itself loving God and, at the same time, is conscious not only of that love but also of humility and reverence, it is a sign of the working of the Holy Spirit.

CHAPTER 30

THE SUBTLE NATURE OF INTERIOR WORDS

Locutions or interior words can be so subtle or deceptive that even a prudent soul is led astray. The experience should be related to a competent director and his or her advice should be followed. If such an expert director is not available, it is better to ignore these words entirely, repeating them to nobody. The soul should attach no importance to these things in any way. If they come from God, then he will see to their fruition.

CHAPTER 31

THE WORD OF GOD

Sometimes the Lord can speak to the soul in such a substantial way that what he says immediately has its effect. Thus if he should say, "Fear not," the soul would immediately be without fear. God's word is full of power and what he says to the soul, he produces. One of his words works greater good within the soul than all that the soul itself has done throughout its life. These words are never given for the purpose of having the soul perform some activity.

The soul should neither desire nor refrain from desiring such words from God. It should neither reject them nor fear them. Let the soul simply be resigned and humble with respect to them. There is no need to fear deception in regard to such words nor to be concerned with the mind misunderstanding them. Neither the world, the flesh nor the devil can mimic these words of God or their effects. These words are greatly conducive to the union of the soul with God. Happy is the soul who experiences such words.

☙

Chapter 32

Gifts of God

God grants what favors he wills to whom he wills and for whatever reason he wills. Sometimes he will touch the soul and its will in such a way that understandings and knowledge and intelligence overflows from them into the intellect. These feelings are produce passively in the soul by God's grace alone. The soul should remain in a state of complete receptivity. Once again the soul should neither desire nor reject such an experience but simply remain resigned, humble and passive.

THE ASCENT OF MOUNT CARMEL:
BOOK THE THIRD

Chapter 1

Hope and Love, Memory and Will

We have completed our treatment of the intellect or the understanding and its relation to the supernatural virtue of faith. Now we treat of the memory and the will and their relation to the supernatural virtues of hope and love. All three depend upon one another and having treated of faith already, we have gone a great part of the way in treating of hope and love.

Chapter 2

Rejecting the Natural Faculties

Our faculties of memory and will must recede into the background and be put to silence so that God may, of his own accord, work divine union in the soul. The soul must proceed in its growing knowledge of God by learning that which he is not, rather than that which he is. This is what is called the apophatic experience. It means an experience without any shape or form whatsoever. It consists in renouncing and rejecting everything that it is possible to renounce in regard to the faculties whether it be natural or supernatural.

We shall begin with the memory. We shall draw it out from its natural state and limitations and cause it to rise above itself. Only in this way can it attain to the supreme hope of God. The memory has a natural knowledge which is formed by way of objects from the five senses. The soul must empty itself of this kind of knowledge, whether direct or through the imagination, and remain barren and bare as if these forms had never passed through it. To be united to God, the memory must be totally separated from all forms which are not God.

When this occurs through the grace of God, this oblivion of the memory and suspension of the imagination may reach a point where the soul transcends even time and any knowledge of what occurs during that transcended time. There is no thought, no imagination, no feeling and no memory. It is to be noted that these suspensions belong to the beginnings of union with God but do not come to pass in those who are perfect in this union.

This experience is not to be seen as an obliteration of our faculties but as an elevation of them. For beginners in this experience, the soul will fall into great oblivion with respect to all of its senses and knowledge. It will be very negligent concerning its outward behavior, at times forgetting to eat or drink, and being uncertain if it has done this or not. This is because of the absorption of the memory in God. However, once the soul attains to the habit of union, it no longer has these periods of oblivion. When the memory is transformed in God, it passes beyond natural limitations and God is the entire master of it. It is God who moves and commands according to his Holy Spirit and will. As St. Paul says, "He that is joined unto God becomes one spirit with him."

In this state the soul, to all outward appearances, is completely normal. It lives and moves and performs the activities of its life outwardly just as others do. It sleeps and wakes, works and recreates, eats and drinks, and does all the things it had previously been want to do. However, now it is driven or operated, as it were, by the divine activity. It is God in whom the soul now lives and moves and has its being. It wills only what God wills. It does only what God wishes it to do. It remembers what God wishes it to remember.

We are speaking here of what is called the active night and purification of the soul. It is basically the work of God but the memory may place itself actively, as far as lies in its power, in this situation. The spiritual person must habitually exercise caution in this way. He or she must allow him- or herself to forget everything that comes to his or her memory. As another great mystical work, "The Cloud of Unknowing," tells us, "We must bury everything beneath a cloud of forgetting." In this way the memory is left free and disencumbered and tied to no consideration at all. Of what use is natural memory in supernatural matters. It is a hindrance rather than a help.

In the beginning the suspension of the memory and other forms of knowledge will occur only at times of deep prayer—that is, in contemplation. This should not discourage the spiritual soul. Through patience and hope, God will not fail to come to its aid. Gradually, our contemplative prayer will become a contemplative attitude. And the effects of which we speak will extend throughout one's day. More and more, the soul will experience that it is in God that we live and move and have our being. We shall then be able to say with St. Paul, "I live now, not I but Christ lives in me."

CHAPTER 3

THE FIRST PROBLEM

There are three kinds of evil or problems the soul must face here in its journey to God. The first problem comes from the world. The memory, as it is stepping into this spiritual darkness, will naturally cling to things which it has heard, seen, touched, etc., through the senses. Imperfections and downright venial sins such as the memory of pain, fear, hatred, vainglory, critical and unloving judgements of others, etc., will arise in the soul. Some of these things are so subtle and minute that the soul clings to them without even realizing it. It is necessary to conquer these once and for all by denying the memory completely, even of good thoughts and meditations upon God.

By shutting the door of the memory to all things, whether from above or below, we cause it to become still and dumb and the ear of the spirit to become attentive in silence to God alone. We then become an embodiment of the saying of the Prophet, "Speak, Lord, for your servant hears." When the soul closes the doors of its faculties, memory, understanding and will, the Lord will enter through those closed doors just as he did for the disciples on Easter Sunday. Wait in prayer in detachment and emptiness, for the Lord will not tarry, he will come soon.

CHAPTER 4

THE SECOND PROBLEM, OR EVIL

The devil can continually bring to the memory new kinds of knowledge and reflections with which he can introduce pride, avarice, wrath, envy, etc. When the memory shuts the door to everything, it shuts the door also to these evils. The memory can retain many kinds of sadness and affliction and vain and evil joys, both with respect to thoughts about God and also to things of the world. Many impurities thus rooted in our souls. We are thus distracted from the highest recollection, which consists in fixing the whole soul upon the one incomprehensible God.

CHAPTER 5

THE THIRD PROBLEM

The natural understandings of the memory can hinder moral good and deprive us of spiritual good. Moral good consists in restraining disorderly desires which results in tranquility and peace and the moral virtues. This restraining cannot be accomplished unless the soul forgets and withdraws itself from those things whence arise the affections. When all things are forgotten, no disturbances can arise in the soul through the memory. Whenever the soul remembers anything, it is moved or disturbed much or little according to the nature of that memory. So it is lacking in moral tranquility.

And encumbered memory also hinders spiritual good. Spiritual good impresses itself only upon souls that are restrained and at peace. The soul that is preoccupied with the things of the memory is not free to attend to the incomparable things of God.

CHAPTER 6

THE BENEFITS OF EMPTINESS

When the soul empties itself and forgets all of the apprehensions of the memory, it enjoys tranquility and peace of mind. Thus it is amply prepared for acquiring divine and human wisdom and the virtues. It is also freed from suggestions of the devil which come through thoughts and ideas that the memory may retain. The soul is then prepared to be moved by the Holy Spirit and taught by him. It can bear everything with peaceful tranquility and allows the soul, in the midst of its adversities, to form a true judgment about them and to find a fitting remedy.

⁓

CHAPTER 7

THE IMAGINATION

The memory has a particular attraction for visions, revelations, locutions and feelings which come in a supernatural way. It often retains the impression of these things very vividly. The soul should not reflect upon the remembrances of these things even when they are supernatural. The more it does so, the less capacity it has for entering into the darkness of faith. These remembrances are not God. If the soul is to reach union with God it must empty itself of all that is not God. To possess such memories is contrary to hope because hope belongs to that which is not possessed. The more the memory rejects these things, the greater is its hope. The more the memory has of hope, the more it has of union with God. Some souls will not deprive themselves of the sweetness which memory finds in these forms and notions. They deny themselves then of the perfect sweetness and the supreme possession of God. One that renounces not all that one has cannot be the disciple of Christ. When the soul is engaged in contemplative prayer, it must very deliberately reject the memory of everything, even holy and supernatural things.

❧

Chapter 8

Knowledge of Supernatural Things

There are any number of evil results that can afflict the soul by clinging to the memory of supernatural experiences. It is easy for the soul to be deceived in its judgment regarding these things as it reflects upon them. If the soul makes mistakes in respect to natural memories, how much more is it apt to err in regard to supernatural ones? Sometimes they may not even come from God. They may be false and misleading. Even the ones that are true may be mistakenly thought to be false. The imagination may give them qualities they do not have or may take from them qualities they should have. It is best then for the spiritual person not to reflect upon such things or apply one's judgment to them. Any concerns should be brought to one's spiritual father.

Chapter 9

Self-esteem and Presumption

The spiritual soul may attribute these supernatural experiences of the memory to God. It may hold itself unworthy of them and give God thanks for them. Nevertheless, there often remains in it spirit a certain secret satisfaction and self-esteem from which, without the soul's knowing it, there will come great spiritual pride. This may be observed by the aversion which arises in it when others do not praise its spirituality on the experiences it enjoys. The soul is also mortified when others tell it they have the same experiences or even superior ones. This arises from secret self-esteem and pride. This may be present in the soul even when there is a certain degree of awareness of its own wretchedness. It resembles in spirit the Pharisee who thanked God that he was not like other men. The soul should realize that all visions, revelations and feelings which come from heaven, and any thoughts proceeding from these, are of less worth than the least act of humility. To be free then the soul must forget these supernatural experiences.

CHAPTER 10

A FURTHER PROBLEM

The soul can be corrupted and bewildered by the sweetness caused by these apprehensions of the memory. The result can be spiritual gluttony. More importance then is given to these things than is given to the detachment and emptiness which are found in faith, hope and love. This may start out as a very small error but, like the grain of mustard seed, it will soon grow into a tall tree.

❧

CHAPTER 11

PERFECT HOPE

For the soul to come to union with God in hope, it must renounce every possession of the memory. For hope in God to be perfect there must be nothing in the memory that is not God. So if the memory desires to pay heed to anything, past or present, natural or supernatural, it hinders the soul from reaching God.

CHAPTER 12

THE BEING OF GOD

God is incomprehensible. Nothing that exists in our memory can remotely approximate his greatness. It is natural for the soul to hold in esteem those things in its memory and intellect which it sees as being made in the image of God. This leads it to make a certain inward comparison between such things and God. This, in turn, can prevent it from judging in esteeming God as highly as it should. Anything that can be encompassed by the faculties of the soul, however lofty they be in this life, have no comparison with the being of God. True hope can only come about by the realization that God is completely Other.

❧

CHAPTER 13

BENEFITS

There are great benefits that come from emptying the imagination of all forms and images. There is a great feeling of rest and quiet because there is no anxiety. There is nothing to be anxious about, either naturally or supernaturally. The soul is given freedom in regard to the time and energy it would have wasted in dealing with these things. This practice will also facilitate our approach to union with God. God has no image, nor form nor figure, and when we desire to strip ourselves of all forms, we come closer to God. An objection may be raised that many spiritual persons try to profit by the communication and feelings which they receive from God. Even though God sends these things they must be rejected and cast aside. God gives it for a good reason and it will have a good effect. But this will be due to God, not to ourselves. He will produce passively in the soul immediately what he wishes, without any work of our own. We do not even have to will to receive them. We must do absolutely nothing. This is equivalent to rejecting immediately any forms or images given to the memory.

This actually preserves the graces which God gives in this manner because, by not accepting them, we do not interfere or distort them in any way. Any work that the soul does on these images would be natural, subject to error and of our own choosing. Thus we will hinder the communication which God is giving us, and even undoing it. We must let go and let God. When God acts on the memory, he is moving the soul to things which are above its own power and knowledge. By applying its own faculties to these things, the soul interferes with them and even destroys the effects God wishes to give through them.

Chapter 14

The Memory and Spiritual Knowledge

When the soul has had an experience of one of these spiritual apprehensions in its intellect or will, it can easily remember them. This is all right when these memories produce good effects. When the effects produced on the soul are those of light, love, joy and spiritual fervor they should be embraced without fear.

Chapter 15

Spiritual Memory and Hope

Our aim here is the union of the soul with God through the memory in hope. We can only hope for something we do not have, and the less we have, the greater our capacity for hoping. On the other hand, the more we possess (even of spiritual images, etc.) the less capacity there is for hoping and the less room, as it were, there will be for God. Should these memories oblige us to perform some duty, then we should do so but without setting any affection upon the memories themselves. In this way they will produce no effect in the soul.

It must be understood that we are here speaking of images in the mind only. It is the teaching of the church that external images such as paintings, relics, statues, etc., are holy and worthy. But even then their purpose is to allow us to pass beyond them to the spiritual realities they signify.

CHAPTER 16

THE DARK NIGHT OF THE WILL

We have spoken of the purgation of the understanding in order to ground it in the virtue of faith. We have also spoken of the purgation of the memory in order to ground it in the virtue of hope. We will now speak of the purgation of the will in order to ground it in the virtue of charity. Without charity there is no hope or faith. We will now treat of the active detachment or, as we say, the dark night of the will, to make it perfect in the virtue of the love of God. In chapter 6 of Deuteronomy, Moses says: "Thou shalt love the Lord your God with your whole heart and with your whole soul and with your whole strength." Herein is contained all that is necessary for union with God through the will by means of love.

Moses is telling the soul to employ all of its faculties, its desires, operations and affections in God. The power of the soul consists in its faculties, passions and desires, all of which are ruled by the will. Now when these powers are directed by the will toward God and turned away from all that is not God, then the soul loves God with all of its strength.

In order for the will to love God with all its strength, it must be purged from its unruly operations, affections and desires. These unruly passions are four, namely: joy, hope (for anything less than God), grief and fear. It is clear when these passions are directed toward God all the power of the soul is likewise directed. Thus the soul must rejoice in only that which is for the honor and glory of God, it must hope for nothing else, it must not grieve except for things that concern this, and it must not fear anything except God alone. If the soul rejoices in anything other than God, the less will it rejoice in God. If it hopes for anything other than God, the less it will hope in God, and so with the other passions.

The whole business of attaining to union with God consists in purging the will from its unruly affections and desires. Then it will no longer be a base, human will, but may become a divine will, being made one with the will of God. When the will is dependent on creatures and rejoices in things that do not merit rejoicing, in hopes and things which bring no profit, it grieves over things over which it should rejoice, and fears where there is no reason for fearing. As they are less attached to God then, these unruly passions have a greater dominion over the soul. From this there arise in the soul vices and imperfections. On the other hand, when these are under control there arise in the soul all the virtues. These four passions of the soul are so intimately united to one another that, if one of them is ordered by reason the rest will become so likewise. So if one is recollected, the other three will be recollected. If one hopes or rejoices, the other three will do so likewise. The reverse is also true. If one of these passions is disordered, the others will be disordered also. So if joy, hope, fear and grief are allowed to be in the soul in a disordered way that is not directed to God, they will not allow the soul to remain in that peace which is necessary for the wisdom it is capable of receiving from God.

CHAPTER 17

THE FIRST OF THESE AFFECTIONS, JOY

Joy is the satisfaction of the will together with esteem for something which it considers desirable. Joy may be active or passive. Active joy arises when the soul clearly understands the reason for its rejoicing and when it is in its own power to rejoice or not. Joy is passive when the soul does not have a clear understanding of its reason or does understand this but it is not in the soul's power to rejoice or not. We will speak now of active joy that is voluntary and distinct.

Joy may arise from six kinds of blessings, namely: temporal, natural, sensual, moral, supernatural and spiritual. The will must not be encumbered by any of these because it should place the strength of its joy in God. There is one principle truth that we must understand here. In the light of this truth we should see, understand, and direct our joy in all these blessings to God. The truth is this. The will must never rejoice in anything except that which is to the honor and glory of God and that the greatest honor we can show God is to serve him according to the Gospels. Anything less than this is of no value.

Chapter 18

Joy in Temporal Blessings

By temporal blessings we understand riches, rank, office, children, relatives, marriages, etc.: all those things wherein the will may rejoice. It is in vain for the soul to rejoice in these things. Riches and titles are to be rejoiced in only if they make the soul a better servant of God. While not in themselves evil, it is very difficult to rejoice in them purely for the service of God.

Also there is no cause for rejoicing in children because they are many, or rich, or endowed with natural talents, but only if they serve God. It is also vanity to rejoice in a marriage to the degree that it is unclear whether or not it will enable us to serve God better. This is true of every temporal blessing. St. Paul warns us that the time is short. They who have wives should be as if they had none. They who weep should be as them that weep not. They that rejoice as them that rejoice not. They that buy as them that possess not. They that use this world as them that use it not. He says this to show us that we must not rejoice over anything except things that tend to the service of God.

CHAPTER 19

DANGERS OF REJOICING ON TEMPORAL THINGS

A tiny spark of fire, if it be not quenched, may enkindle great fires which set the world ablaze. So when the will sets its affections upon temporal blessings, even from very small beginnings, great evils may arise. All blessings come to the soul when it is united with God by the affection of its will. Also, when it withdraws itself from God because of creature affection, all evils proportionately will arise.

There are four degrees of this evil. There is a blunting of the mind with regard to God, a clouding of the intellect and the judgment. Even holiness will not save a soul if it gives way to rejoicing in temporal things because its clear and alert judgment will be obscured. The second degree of evil arises from this when the will is driven toward creatures with greater abandon. Thus it withdraws itself from the things of God and devotes itself to follies. The will withdraws more and more from justice and virtues as it reaches out more and more in affection for creatures. They are not free from malice as are those in the first degree.

The third degree of this evil is a complete falling away from God and a relapse into mortal sin through greed for worldly things. They become children of this world who can never be satisfied because they have withdrawn from the only source of satisfaction which is God. As Jeremiah says: "They have forsaken me, who am the fountain of living water and they have dug to themselves broken cisterns that can hold no water."

The fourth degree of evil follows from this. Such a soul departs far from God according to it memory, understanding and will, forgetting him as though he were not it God. This happens because the soul has made for itself a God of money and of temporal blessings. Such souls will subject God and the things of God to temporal things. They will serve the Mammon rather than God. They dedicate their lives to worldly goods as their personal god. They will discover how wretched is the reward such a god as theirs will bestow. It will only lead to despair and death. Nothing will bring them satisfaction because our hearts can find satisfaction only in God. The Scriptures tell us: "Be not afraid when a man shall be made rich: that is, envy him not, that he outstrips you, for when he dies he shall carry nothing away, neither shall his glory nor his joy descend with him."

CHAPTER 20

JOY IN TEMPORAL THINGS

When the soul rejects its joy in temporal things, it frees its heart from them. Caution must be taken that this is necessary even in small things. Small things become great things before we know it, and then it becomes almost impossible to divorce ourselves from them. Even if this is not done for the sake of Christian perfection, it should be done because of the temporal advantages that result from it. By doing this, covetousness gives way to liberality, one of the principal attributes of God. The soul will acquire liberty of soul, charity of reason, rest, peaceful confidence in God and true reverence. It will even find greater joy in creatures through its detachment from them. It cannot rejoice in them if it is attached. Attachment is an anxiety that, like a bond, ties the spirit down to the earth.

Being detached from the joy of temporal things does not mean we reject them or the joy. If we can look upon temporal things without the anxiety of detachment, we can enjoy them but in a very different way. We enjoy them according to their substance and their truth which the senses alone cannot grasp. We possess them as not possessing, as St. Paul says. Being detached from the joy leaves the judgment clear, even as the mists leave the air clear when they are scattered.

The soul that desires a certain degree of joy in creatures must have an equal degree of disquietude and grief in its heart which results from this. The soul that is detached is untroubled, in prayer or apart from it, from anxieties and thus it is able to store up great treasures in heaven. The soul must take joy only in its service of God, and in its striving for God's glory in all things. It must direct all things to this end and turn aside from vanity in them, looking on them neither for its own joy not for its consolation.

By detachment from creatures the heart is left free for God. This is a disposition necessary for all spiritual favors.

❧

Chapter 21

It Is Vain to Rejoice in the Good Things of Nature

The soul must direct itself by means of these things to God. Natural blessings in the body are beauty, grace, bodily constitution and all other bodily endowments. In the soul they are good understanding, discretion and other things that pertain to reason. God bestows these so that we may better know and love him. To rejoice in them for their own sake is vanity and deception. As Solomon says: "Grace is deceitful and beauty is vain; the woman who fears God, she shall be praised." He also says, "Vanity of vanities and all is vanity except to love God and serve him." The spiritual person must purge his or will lest he or she engage in vain rejoicing over these temporal things. Natural gifts come from the earth and will return to it. They should be used only to direct the heart to God with rejoicing and gladness because God himself has all these beauties and graces in the most eminent degree.

❧

CHAPTER 22

BEWARE OF REJOICING IN THE GOOD THINGS OF NATURE

There are many spiritual and bodily evils which come to the soul when it sets its rejoicing on the good things of nature. When we set our heart on something we esteem, we withdraw it from other things. It is easy then to fall into contempt for all these other things.

We have spoken of detachment from joy in temporal things; we now speak of detachment from joy in things of nature. But things of nature are more closely connected with who we are then are temporal possessions. Attachment to them deadens the senses, clouds the reason and judgment and distracts the mind. From this follows lukewarmness and weakness of spirit which finds the things of God tedious and troublesome and even abhorrent. Let us remember how vain and dangerous it is to rejoice in anything save the service of God. Let us remember how many evils come to people daily through this vanity. Let us remember how many, even in the Church's hierarchy, drink this cup of vanity, how many rulers of nations are stupefied and bewildered by it. Let us remember the numerous deaths it causes, the loss of honor, the commission of insults, the dissipation of wealth, the strife, adultery, rape and fornication, and the fall of many, great and small alike.

❧

Chapter 23

Benefits Received By Not Rejoicing in the Good Things of Nature

These benefits include making a way for humility and a general charity toward neighbors. By not rejoicing in the good things of nature, the soul is free from deceit to and able to love them all rationally and spiritually. No one should be loved except because of the virtue that is in him or her. This is pleasing to God and brings great freedom. Even if there is attachment involved, there is greater attachment to God. The greater our attachment or love for God, the greater becomes our love for our neighbor.

The soul that sets its rejoicing upon the good things of nature can never deny itself as our Savior councils. One who renounces this kind of rejoicing brings great tranquility to the soul and recollection to the senses and empties them of distraction. Evil things do not make an impression upon such souls and its renunciation results in spiritual cleanness of body and soul. This is how the body becomes a temple of the Holy Spirit. The soul is delivered from countless vanities and many other evils both spiritual and temporal. Finally there follows a generosity of the soul which is as necessary to the service of God as is liberty of spirit. Temptations are easily vanquished, trials faithfully endured, and virtues flourish.

CHAPTER 24

ANOTHER PURGING

We have spoken about the soul and its joy in attachment to temporal things and to things of nature. We will now treat of rejoicing with respect to the good things of sense. We mean by this everything in this life that can be apprehended by the senses of sight, hearing, smell, taste or touch, and by imaginary reflections on all of these things. From this rejoicing in sensible objects, we must darken the will and purge it from them and, instead, direct it to God by means of them.

In order to do this we must understand that the senses belong to the lower part of a person and they can neither know nor understand God as God is. The eye cannot see him or anything that is like him. The ear cannot hear his voice or any sound that resembles it. The sense of smell cannot perceive a perfume so sweet as he. The taste cannot detect or savor anything so sublime. The touch cannot feel a movement so delicate and full of delight. Neither can his form or any figure that represents him enter into the imagination. It is vain for the will to rejoice upon pleasure caused by any of these senses. To do so would be to hinder the power of the will from occupying itself with God and rejoicing in him alone.

The will then must not rest upon these things. However, when the will does find pleasure in things of the senses, and as a result soars upward to rejoice in God, this is very good.

There are indeed souls who are greatly moved by objects of the sense to seek God. Care must be taken, however, by spiritual persons who indulge in such recreations of the sense. They may use them as a pretext of offering devotion to God in a way that is really recreation and not prayer, a way which gives more pleasure to themselves than to God.

When a soul does find that pleasure in things of the senses and the thought and affection of its will is at once centered upon God because of them, it is good. It should take no pleasure in the things themselves save the pleasure it receives from being centered upon God through them. Thus do things of the senses serve the purpose for which God created them, that he should be better known and loved because of them. When such pleasures are taken away and the soul mourns for them, it is a sign that it was taking pleasure in them for their own sake and not for God.

Chapter 25

Desire for Good Things of the Senses

The soul must reject the joy which arises from things of the senses and direct its rejoicing to God. If it does not do so, many evils may follow: darkness in the reason, lukewarmness, spiritual weariness, etc. The soul that does not deny itself joy in visible things is subjected to vanity of spirit and distraction of the mind, unruly covetousness, immodesty, impurity of thought and envy. The soul that does not reject joy in hearing useless things is subjected to gossiping, envy, rash judgment and many other evils. The soul that does not reject joy in sweet perfumes is subject to loathing of the poor and spiritual insensibility. The soul that does not reject joy in eating and drinking is subjected to gluttony and drunkenness, wrath, discord and want of charity with the poor. Also spiritual torpor can result and a corruption of the desire for spiritual things. The soul that does not reject joy in the sense of touch is subject to sensible softness and a predisposition to sin and evil. The remaining senses are blunted also according to the measure of this desire. Judgment is put to confusion. Darkness of the soul and weakness of the heart is begotten. Reason is weakened and affected in such a way that it cannot offer good counsel.

When the soul denies itself in rejoicing in temporal things there are many benefits. It is recollected in God. Its virtues are preserved and even increased. The sensual becomes spiritual, the animal becomes rational, a human life becomes angelical, and instead of being temporal and human, it becomes celestial and divine. When a person rejoices in things of the sense he or she is sensual. When he or she lifts his or her rejoicing above things of the sense he or she is celestial. When the sensual power is diminished, the spiritual power is increased. St. Paul calls the sensual person the animal person who perceives not the things of God. But the person who lifts up his or her will to God, he calls the spiritual person, saying that this person penetrates and judges all things, even the deep things of God. Yet another benefit is that the pleasures of the will in temporal matters is greatly increased. The Savior says that they shall receive a hundred-fold even in this life. The opposite is also true. For if one takes joy in things of the sense, one shall have a hundredfold of affliction and misery.

When joy in the senses is purged, spiritual joy is the result. To the soul that is pure all things are pure, even the things of the senses. When a soul lives a spiritual life, and modifies the animal life, it journeys straight to God. All of its actions are spiritual and pertain to the life of the spirit. Hence it follows that such a person, being pure in heart, finds in all things a knowledge of God which is joyful, chaste and spiritual.

For a person to withdraw his or her soul from the life of the sense, he or she must deny him- or herself joy with respect to sensual powers and so habituate his or her senses to be directed to God. That which is born of the flesh is flesh, and that which is born of the Spirit is spirit. The soul that has not yet mortified its pleasure in things of the sense must take great care with respect to them. They will not help a person to become more spiritual as he or she would like to think. For the powers of his or her soul to increase, a person must quench the joy and desire that he or she finds in sensible things. This dark night, or purgation of the senses, will even result in an increase in the glory of the soul in heaven. For every momentary, fleeting joy that has been renounced, St. Paul says, there shall be laid up in heaven an exceeding weight of glory.

❧

CHAPTER 26

MORAL GOODS

We have seen now that the soul must be purged of joy in temporal, sensible and spiritual goods. We will now consider moral goods. By these we understand the practice of the virtues, such as the works of mercy, observing the laws of God and humans, and the practice of all good intentions and inclinations. The will may rejoice in these practices more than in any of the three other kinds previously mentioned.

Moral goods bring with them peace and an ordered use of reason. These virtues deserve to be esteemed, humanly speaking, for their own sake. Thus a person may well rejoice in the possession of them. They bring blessings in human and temporal form. For this reason even pagan philosophers and wise men esteemed and praised them and endeavored to possess and practice them.

The Christian should rejoice in the moral goods that he or she possesses, even in the temporal good and his or her temporal blessings. But he or she must not stop here. Because the Christian has the light of faith by which he or she hopes for eternal life, he or she must rejoice in the possession of moral good because by doing these works for the love of God, he or she will gain eternal life. Thus the Christian should set his or her eyes and rejoicing on serving and honoring God with his or her good customs and virtues.

Many Christians today have virtues and practice good works which will not profit them for eternal life, because they have not sought in them the glory and honor which belongs to God alone. The Christian must rejoice, not in performing good works, but in doing them for the love of God alone. He or she must realize that the value of these good works, fast, alms, penances, etc., depends upon the love of God which inspires him or her to do them. Thus they are more excellent because they are performed with a pure and sincere love of God rather than in self-interest, consolation, or praise. The soul must desire to serve God in its good works and purge itself from lesser desires, remaining in darkness with respect to them.

CHAPTER 27

SEVEN EVILS

There are seven evils into which a soul may fall through vain rejoicing in its good works. They are all the more hurtful because they are spiritual. The first evil is vanity. The soul cannot rejoice in its works without esteeming them. From this arises boasting as is said of the Pharisee who congratulated himself before God because he fasted and did good works.

The second evil is connected with this. It consists of judging ourselves by comparison with others. They come off as inferior and imperfect when we think their good works are inferior to our own. As a result, we esteem them less. This evil the Pharisee practiced in his prayer when he said: "I thank you that I am not as other men are, robbers and adulterers."

The third evil is that because they look for pleasure in their good works, they perform them only when they see that some pleasure or praise will result from them. They do things so that they may be seen by others and do not work for the love of God. The fourth evil follows from this. Since they desire to have joy or consolation or honor in this life, as a result of their good works, they will receive no reward in heaven.

There is great misery among people because of this evil. Many good works performed in public are of no value to those who do them because they are not detached from their temporal rewards. What else can we think of the memorials which certain people set up to commemorate their own good works? They even set them up in the very churches, as if they wish to place themselves instead of images in places where all bend the knee? Are they not worshiping themselves more than God? These are the worst cases but still others wish to be praised, thanked or renowned for their good works by having an intermediary perform them so they may be the better known. This is the sounding of trumpets which, the Savior says in the Gospel, vain men do, and for which reason they shall have no reward from God to flee from such evil, and the soul must hide its good works, even from itself, so that God alone may see them. This is what Jesus meant when he said: "Let not your left hand know what your right hand does."

The fifth evil is that such persons make no progress on the road of perfection. If they need to find consolation in their good works, it follows that when no consolation is found in them, they will not persevere. The sixth evil is that such persons deceive themselves. They think that the good works which give them pleasure must be better than those that do not. The contrary is true. Works in which a person is mortified are acceptable and precious to God by reason of self-denial.

The seventh evil is that a person becomes incapable of receiving reasonable counsel with regard to the good works that he or she should perform. He or she is greatly weakened in charity toward God and neighbor. The self-love contained in his or her good works causes his or her charity to grow cold.

Chapter 28

Further Moral Goods

The soul benefits greatly when it does not set joy on moral goods. It is freed from many deceptive temptations involved in this rejoicing. Vain rejoicing is itself deception, as is boasting. Without the passion of joy and pleasure, the soul can perform good works with greater deliberation and perfection. Acting under the influence of pleasure, the soul becomes inconsistent. Also wrath and concupiscence become strong and do not submit to reason. If the joy which such persons have in their work is the strength of the work, then when the joy is quenched, the work ceases. The wise person sets his or her eyes upon the benefit of his or her work, not upon his or her pleasure. Then he or she can derive from his or her work a stable joy. Also when vain joy in good works is quenched, the soul becomes poor in spirit. Blessed are the poor in spirit, for theirs is the kingdom of heaven. Such a soul will be prudent in its actions. It will not act in haste but meekly and humbly. It will become pleasing to God and humans, free from spiritual sloth and greed and from a thousand other vices.

CHAPTER 29

SUPERNATURAL GOOD

Supernatural gifts are graces given by God which transcend natural capacity. Such gifts are wisdom and knowledge which God gave to Solomon. They are also the graces St. Paul speaks of: faith, healing, working of miracles, prophecy, knowledge, discernment of spirits, interpretation of words and the gift of tongues. They are similar to spiritual gifts but they are practiced on behalf of humans. This is why God gives them. Spiritual gifts have to do with God and the soul alone. Supernatural gifts may result in temporal or spiritual blessings. Temporal blessings are the healing of the sick, prophesying concerning the future, etc. By performing these good works, God is known and served. Thus they have a spiritual benefit. A person should rejoice in these graces only once he or she reaps from them the spiritual fruit of serving God with true charity.

CHAPTER 30

REJOICING IN SUPERNATURAL GOOD

Three principal evils may come to the soul that rejoices in supernatural good. It may deceive and be deceived by such joy which blunts and obscures the judgment. Also when the soul has joy in these things, it becomes eager for them and seeks to practice them out of season. Thus the soul does not understand them as it should and does not profit by them as it should. The soul may even seek to acquire them by immoral and sacrilegious means. And so it counterfeits the true spiritual and supernatural gifts of God. From this evil may proceed a second, a falling away from the faith. Sometimes too great an account is taken of these things and the soul ceases to lean upon the substantial practice of the virtue of faith.

~

Chapter 31

Two Benefits

When a soul is delivered from the evils previously mentioned by renouncing joy in the matter of supernatural graces, it acquires two benefits. First, it magnifies and exalts God, and it exalts itself. God is exalted in the soul by withdrawing the heart from all that is not God. The soul thus centers itself in God alone who then bears witness of who he himself is. As David said: "Be still and know that I am God." Secondly, the soul is exalted in purest faith when it withdraws from all desire for signs and testimonies. At the same time, God increases in it charity and hope.

Chapter 32

Another Kind of Good

There is another kind of good (the sixth we have mentioned). These are the good things of the spirit which are all those things that influence and aid the soul in divine things in its intercourse with God, and the communications of God to the soul. They may be sweet or painful. They may also be clearly understood or understood only in a dark or confused manner. They may pertain to the understanding, to the will or to the imagination (memory). We will speak now only of those clear and distinct sweet blessings.

Chapter 33

Good Things of the Spirit

We have already spoken of the good things of the spirit which can be given to the understanding and the memory. We ask now how the will is to behave regarding rejoicing in these things. Actually, this has already been treated previously. Whenever we spoke of the understanding and the memory purging themselves of attachment to spiritual things, we also understand that the will does likewise. The understanding, the memory, and the imagination cannot admit or reject anything unless the will consents. So the same teaching that serves from the one will serve for the other.

~

Chapter 34

The Will and Good Things

There are four goods which cause joy to the will. The first involves images, portraits of saints, and religious items such as rosaries, crucifixes, etc. These are useful for divine worship and they move the will to devotion. Our wills should rejoice in what they represent rather than in the items themselves. When they move us to devotion, they serve this purpose and are beneficial. Our eyes should be fixed on their devotional value rather than on the intricacies of their workmanship or on their material value.

Care should be taken that we do not treat these images as things of value in themselves. We should not take pride in their ownership. We should not embellish them with precious jewels or metals or, God forbid, clothe them as though we were playing with dolls. We should beware of collecting images, comparing and matching them to one another, or proclaiming their value or artistic merit. Possessed in this way, they are nothing but idols.

The truly devout person needs few images and chooses those that harmonize with the devotion they are supposed to inspire rather than with worldly fashions and tastes. His or her heart is not attached to these images, and if they are taken from him or her, he or she grieves very little.

Care is to be taken especially with rosaries. Many, if not most, people have some weakness with regard to them. They are more concerned with their workmanship, color or metal or other decorations than with the devotion they are intended to inspire. It is troubling to see even spiritual persons so greatly attached to the workmanship of such things. They amount to nothing more than temporal attachments.

Chapter 35

Ignorance and Images

Many persons display an amazing stupidity with regard to images. Some of them place more confidence in one kind of image than in another even when both represent the same thing, such as Christ or Our Lady. It is not a statue that we should be concerned with but the faith and purity of heart of the one who prays. It is true God sometimes grants more favors by means of one image rather than by another of the same kind. This is only because one may arouse more devotion than another.

So God may work miracles by means of one kind of image rather than another. This does not mean one is better than another. It does mean that one inspires more devotion than the other. God does not work miracles because of the image, which is no more than a painted thing, but because of the devotion and faith which the one who prays before the image has. When there is devotion and faith, any image will suffice. If there is no devotion and faith, none will suffice.

CHAPTER 36

DIRECTED TO GOD

I mages are of great benefit for remembering God and the saints and for moving the will to devotion. They can also lead to great error, even when supernatural happenings come to pass in connection with them, if the soul should not be able to conduct itself as is fitting for its journey to God. The world, the flesh and the devil may be transformed into an angel of light in order to deceive the soul when it is least prepared. In order to avoid the evils which may happen in this connection, let this general warning suffice in regard to images: strive to set the rejoicing of your will only upon that which the images represent.

~

Chapter 37

Places Dedicated to Prayer

There is a great danger when a soul says that the objects of its rejoicing are holy. A soul feels secure and does not hesitate to become attached to them in a natural way. It can be greatly deceived, thinking itself to be full of devotion because it takes pleasure in holy things. The problem is it is taking pleasure only from its natural desire and temperament and not for the glory of God.

An unfortunate example is found in those who take pleasure in the array with which they betake their oratories. Yet they love God no more in this way than if their oratories were simply adorned. In a lesser way the same unfortunate tendency can be seen in the homes of people where holy objects are given a certain precedence because of their elaborate embellishments or artistic merit.

A similar problem is found where souls rejoice in solemn religious festivals because of the pleasure which they themselves find in it, rather than for the glory it gives to God. The celebration of Christmas is a point at hand. In many instances it has completely lost its religious character. Weddings are another example where the sacramental character of the event is subordinated toward enhancing its secular character by way of elaborate receptions, gifts, etc. Let such souls realize when they act in these ways that they are making festivals in their own honor rather than in that of God. God says of them: "These people honor me with their lips, but their heart is far from me."

CHAPTER 38

HOW HOLY PLACES SHOULD BE USED

Churches, shrines and chapels should be used in order to direct the spirit to God. It is expedient for beginners to find some sensible sweetness in these places since they have not yet detached their desire from things of the world. But the spiritual person must go beyond this. Pure spirituality is bound very little to any of such objects but only to interior recollection and conversation with God. Such a one makes use of images and such places only fleetingly.

To pray best one should choose the place where sense and spirit are least hindered from union with God, a place where God is adored in spirit and in truth. Churches should be places conducive to the recollection of the spirit and not to the senses. Jesus chose solitary places that lifted up the soul to God such as mountains. The truly spiritual person chooses places free from sensible objects and attractions to rejoice in God and be far removed from created things.

❧

Chapter 39

Interior Recollection

To enter perfectly into the true joys of the spirit, the soul must raise its desire for rejoicing above things that are outward and visible, even when these things are holy. To purge the will from vain desire in this matter and to lead it to God, the soul must see to it that its conscience is pure and its will united to God. To do this it should renounce outward things and let go of the pleasures of sensible devotion.

Chapter 40

Sensible Objects and Places

The soul must forget all sensible sweetness in order to enter into true recollection. It should not be jumping from one place to another, from one shrine to another, from one monastery to another. Renunciation of the will and submitting to suffering and inconveniences is necessary to attain spiritual recollection.

❧

CHAPTER 41

PLACES FOR DEVOTION

Places of quiet solitude and gentle surroundings that naturally awaken devotion are beneficial to use providing they lead the will to God and cause it to forget the places themselves. Catering to natural desires and gaining sensible sweetness will only result in spiritual aridity and distraction. Anchorites and holy hermits lived in small cells or caves in the wilderness.

Sometimes there are certain places where God gives to particular people very wonderful spiritual favors. Such places will attract the heart of these people to return to them. It is good to do this if the attraction is free from attachments and the soul's devotion is more keenly awakened.

CHAPTER 42

VARIETY OF CEREMONIES

The great reliance which some souls place in many kinds of ceremonies introduced by uninstructed persons who lack the simplicity of faith is intolerable. This is especially true of ceremonies, seemingly authentic, but which must be performed with such scrupulosity that not a word or gesture can be omitted or added if God is to be served by them. This would include the notion that a mass must be celebrated only at a particular place, or time or have so many candles. If these particulars are not followed nothing is accomplished. What is worse is that some souls desire to feel some effect in themselves, or have their prayers answered, to know that the purpose of the ceremonious prayers will be accomplished. This is the sin of tempting God. They are placing their confidence in something other than God.

CHAPTER 43

DIRECTING THE WILL

Seek first the kingdom of God, and all these other things will be added unto you. This is the key to directing our will in prayer. Some souls pray for their own ends rather than for the glory of God. Because of attachment and vain rejoicing which they have toward something, they multiply their petitions for it. It would be better for them to substitute things of greater importance, such as the cleansing of conscience, purity of heart and their own salvation.

Obviously it is better to direct the energy of our will and our prayer to the things that are most pleasing to God rather than ourselves. When Solomon prayed for wisdom, God responded by giving him not only wisdom but also riches, substance and glory, even though he asked for none of these things. So he will do for us when we direct the strength of our will toward those things that are most pleasing to him.

The soul should not set its will in prayer by way of cer-emonies, prayers and other devotions which do not have the blessings of the church. Take heed of the simplicity in prayer which Christ taught us, the Our Father, with its seven petitions in which are included all our needs, both spiritual and temporal. In these petitions is contained all that is the will of God and all that we need. Remember also than our Lord said that when we pray we should enter into our chamber and shut the door and pray. He also taught us to go to a solitary and deserted place as he did. We can always rely on the instructions of the church as to times, places and methods of prayer.

Chapter 44

Further Vain Rejoicing

Our will may be given vainly also to, what we may call, provocative things. This refers to preachers. It must be pointed out to preachers, if they are to cause their people profit and not encourage vain joy and presumption, that preaching is a spiritual exercise more than a vocal one. It uses outward words but its efficacy resides in the inward spirit. However lofty the doctrine, choice the rhetoric, or sublime the style, it brings no more benefit than is present in the spirit of the preachers.

There also must be proper preparation on the part of their listeners. Not only must the preachers prepare but so must their audience. They must not accept everything they hear simply because it is given in the context of ecclesiastical surroundings. The distortion of God's word, and the thinly disguised greed of modern-day preachers is deplorable. They get a gullible audience because they preach in the name of Jesus, but what they preach is destruction and greed. Preachers should not be listened to who spend more time trying to collect money "for their good works," than in preaching the Gospel of Christ. A good style and gestures and lofty instruction with well-chosen language influence people and produce much effect when accompanied by true spirituality. Without this spirituality even if the sermon gives pleasure and delight to the sense and the understanding, very little of its value remains in the will. We must remember the words of St. Paul: "I, brethren, when I came to you, came not preaching Christ with loftiness of instruction and of wisdom, and my words and my preaching consisted not in the rhetoric of human wisdom, but in the showing forth of the spirit and of the truth."

Here ends the "Ascent to Mount Carmel." The fruit of the preachers is dependent more upon the life they lead than on their distinguished oratorical styles.

❧

THE DARK NIGHT OF THE SOUL
BOOK ONE

ST. JOHN OF THE CROSS

Chapter 1

Beginners

Souls that are beginning the journey to union with God are said to be in the Purgative Way. The usual form of prayer for this Way is verbal or discursive meditation, sometimes called mental prayer. God gradually brings them from this Purgative Way to the state of contemplation, called the Illuminative Way, and finally to the state of perfection called the Unitive Way, begun here, but completed in heaven.

Beginners are weak, like children, and are treated gently by God's grace. Such souls need to understand their feebleness and be encouraged for when God will take them into the dark night where they will be strengthened and prepared for blessed union with Him. In the beginning there is little effort on their part, and they experience great satisfaction in their spiritual exercises. As these souls progress in their conversion, God treats them less and less like weak children and more like adults.

At first, these souls rejoice in spending lengthy periods at prayer. Even penances are pleasurable and spiritual conversations are always consoling. They are conscientious in these practices but, spiritually speaking, they are weak and imperfect. Personal consolations and satisfactions become their motivation. God wants them to love him for his own sake and not for his gifts—that is, the consolations of prayer. They have not been strengthened by the difficult practice of the virtues and so possess many imperfections in the discharge of their spiritual activities. We will look at some of the numerous imperfections found in beginners. It should be noted that a beginner may be any age depending upon the time of his or her conversion to the spiritual journey. Certainly beginners are to be found in religious novitiates and in the early years of seminary training.

CHAPTER 2

IMPERFECTIONS, PRIDE

Pride and complacency is a danger for some of these beginners because they feel so fervent in their spiritual journey. They develop a vain desire to speak of spiritual things and sometimes to instruct rather than be instructed. Sometimes, God forbid, they even set themselves up as spiritual directors. They look down upon others whom they judge to have less devotion than themselves. They are tempted, not by love of God, but by the world, the flesh and the devil to increase their fervor and good works. Thus their virtues become vices. Desiring only themselves to appear holy, they detract from others. They see the splinter in their brother's eye, ignoring the beam in their own. When criticized by their spiritual directors, they feel they are not understood. They will look for another director who will approve their conduct. They will display their devotions openly to be recognized by others, sometimes manifesting them by visible gestures, sighs, etc.

Some want to curry favor with their confessors and so disguise their sins. They exaggerate their virtues and minimize their faults. They are anxious for God to remove their imperfections, but their motive is personal peace rather than love of God. They do not see that acknowledging their faults is a means to avoid pride and presumption. They love to receive praise and dislike praising anyone else. Probably all beginners, at the time of their initial fervor, fall victim to one or other of these imperfections.

Beginners who are truly advancing in perfection act in a completely different way. They place little importance on their deeds and consider everyone else better than they are. Because they are humble, their growing fervor and good deeds cause them to become more aware of what they owe to God and that they are actually unprofitable servants. Knowing their insignificance, they do not seek to have others glorify them with praise. They long to be taught by anyone who can help them and are responsive to all worthwhile advice. They are more eager to speak to their directors of their faults than their virtues. God gives grace to the humble just as he denies it to the proud. When these humble souls fall into imperfections, they suffer this with humility, and with loving fear of God. Few souls are so perfect in the beginning but can do well by avoiding these temptations to pride. Eventually God will take them through the dark night to purify these imperfections.

❧

Chapter 3

Avarice

Sometimes beginners become unhappy because they don't find the consolation they want in spiritual things. Not content with what God gives them, they become greedy. This extends to physical images and rosaries. They prefer one cross to another because of its elaborateness or are constantly exchanging rosaries for more decorative ones. They are decked out in medals and holy objects. Where they go wrong is in their attachment to the number, workmanship, and decoration of these objects rather than to their intrinsic value as aides to devotion. True devotion comes only from the heart and looks to the substance represented by spiritual objects. Any physical attachment to these things must be uprooted if some degree of perfection is to be reached.

The soul must experience the passive purgation of the dark night, which we will soon explain, or it cannot purify itself of these imperfections. But still they should strive to purify and perfect themselves to merit the fruits of this purgation. Nonetheless, no matter how much individual souls do through their own efforts, they cannot purify themselves enough to be disposed for divine union. God must do this.

Chapter 4

LUST

Beginners in the spiritual journey often have what may be called spiritual lust because it proceeds from spiritual things. Impure movements can be experienced in the sensory part of the soul even when the soul is deep in prayer or receiving the sacraments. These may proceed simply from the pleasure that human nature finds in spiritual exercises. The superior part of the soul in prayer experiences renewal and satisfaction in God. The sensual part is ignorant of how to get anything else and so feels a sensual gratification. It takes its share in the experience but only according to its mode which is sensual. This can even happen at the time of communion. However, once the sensory part is reformed through the dark night, it no longer has these infirmities.

The world, the flesh and the devil can also be the source of lust by bringing disquietude to a soul in prayer. Some souls grow slack in their prayer because of this. They attribute undue importance to these thoughts. Some personalities feel they are exposed then to the devil and have no freedom to prevent it. They may require psychological help but ultimately they can be cured by the dark night.

Impure feelings may also arise from the soul's fear of them. It springs up at the sudden remembrance of these thoughts with no fault on their part. Other souls are so delicate that when spiritual gratification is experienced in prayer, they also feel a lust that caresses their senses, again without any fault on their part. This may even extend to certain impure acts. These souls may also experience such feelings when they are involved in any deep-rooted emotion, such as anger or grief.

Some souls acquire a liking for other individuals arising from lust rather than from the spirit. This can be recognized if it is followed by remorse of conscience rather than an increase in the love of God. Affections are purely spiritual if the love of God grows when it grows, or if the love of God is remembered as often as the affection is remembered. Affections proceeding from lust have the contrary effect, making the soul grow cold in the love of God but not without some remorse of conscience. An increased love of God stifles this kind of impure love. That which is born of the flesh is flesh, and that which is born of the Spirit is spirit. This is the difference between these two loves, which enables us to discern one from the other. Love derived from sensuality terminates in sensuality, and the love that is of the spirit terminates in the spirit of God. Also the soul should not ignore common sense remedies, such as consulting with a director, healthy physical exercise and prayer.

All these loves are placed in reasonable order when the soul enters the dark night. It strengthens and purifies love of God and takes away the other. But before that, as we will see, it causes the soul to lose sight of both of them.

❧

CHAPTER 5

ANGER

It is not too long before God removes the first fervor from beginners. He does this because he wants them to love him for himself alone and not for his gifts. Not realizing this, the beginners, deprived of their spiritual consolations, become resentful, peevish and angry. The least little thing sets them off. The soul is not at fault if it does not allow this dejection to influence it. The soul needs the dryness and distress of the dark night to be purged of its resentment.

There is another kind of spiritual anger. Souls can become angry over the sins of others, expressing their resentment and anger. Still other souls, in becoming aware of their own imperfections, grow impatient and angry with themselves. Some make numerous resolutions but since they are not humble, the more they make the more they break, and the greater becomes their anger. They do not have the patience to wait upon God's grace. This lack of spiritual meekness can only be remedied by the purgation of the dark night. Still, on the other hand, there are those who are so patient about their desire for advancement that God would prefer to see them a little less so.

❧

Chapter 6

Spiritual Gluttony

Most beginners fall into some of the imperfections of spiritual gluttony. This happens because of the pleasure beginners find in their spiritual exercises. Some of them strive more for spiritual pleasure than for spiritual purity. They even bring harm to themselves with penances, weakening themselves with fasts without the counsel of spiritual directors. Sometimes they hide these penances and even practice them contrary to obedience. Corporal penance without obedience has no merit and is even harmful. When they cannot avoid obedience they add to it, change it or modify what was commanded. They look only to their self-will and their own desires, thinking that gratifying themselves is serving God.

In their spiritual exercises, they seek personal satisfaction rather than humbly praising God. If they do not have any sensible satisfaction, they think they have accomplished nothing. This is true even with the sacraments. They do not realize that the invisible graces are the greater blessings. This kind of spiritual gluttony is a serious imperfection. When they do not find delight in spiritual exercises, they feel a repugnance to them and sometimes even give them up. They jump from one spiritual exercise to another, always seeking gratification in the things of God. This is why it is important for these beginners to enter the dark night and be purged of this nonsense. Those inclined toward such sensible pleasures in their prayers are usually weak and remiss in carrying the burden of the cross. Sensible pleasure and self-denial are incompatible.

Chapter 7

Sloth and Envy

In regard to envy, some beginners feel sad about the spiritual good of others. They do not want to hear others praised and try to "rain on their parade." They should have rather a holy envy, being sad that they do not have the virtues of others and rejoicing that others do have them.

Regarding spiritual sloth, beginners become weary or bored when they do not find sensible satisfaction in their spiritual practices. They either give them up or go to them begrudgingly. They strive to satisfy their own will rather than God's. These beginners measure God by themselves and not themselves by God. What satisfies them, they think satisfies God. They also become bored when asked to do something unpleasant and are lax in the fortitude that perfection demands. The narrow way of life is not for them.

We can see from all of the imperfections treated so far that beginners need God if they are to advance in the spiritual journey. He must wean them from their gratifications and remove these trivialities and childish ways. Virtues are acquired by very different means. Beginners must realize that no matter how earnest they are and how faithfully they practice the mortification of self, they will be far from it, until God accompanies them by means of the purifying purgation of the dark night.

CHAPTER 8

THE DARK NIGHT

The soul has two parts, a sensory part and a spiritual. Thus there are two kinds of darkness or purgations that occur. One night of purgation is sensory. In this the senses are purged and accommodated to the spirit. The other night is spiritual, in which the spirit is purged and prepared for union with God through love. The sensory night is common and happens to many. The spiritual night only happens to very few. We will speak first of the dark night of the senses.

Since the conduct of beginners in the way of God is much involved in the love of pleasure and self, God desires to withdraw them from this inferior way of loving. He wishes to liberate them from the lowly exercise of the senses and from discursive meditation or mental prayer. In mental prayer they go in search and find him inadequately and with many difficulties but this is necessary in its time and place. This is why beginners, for a period of time, must exercise themselves in the way of cultivating the virtues and by persevering in meditation and prayer. They are, as we say, in the Purgative Way. In this Way they do experience satisfaction in prayer and also they become detached, in some degree, from worldly things and they gain some spiritual strength in God. They become strong enough so that they can endure a certain amount of oppression and dryness necessary for the night of the senses. At this point, God withdraws their delight in spiritual exercises. They find themselves in such darkness that they do not know which way to turn in their discursive meditation. Their interior sensible faculties are immersed in darkness and dryness. God is weaning them from their milk so that they may begin to eat more substantial food. Usually they are quite surprised at this change and do not understand it. This usually happens somewhat quickly to beginners who are fervent in their devotion. Their appetites are being reformed, are being turned away from worldly things. This is necessary in order to enter into the happy, but dark, night of the senses. Usually devout beginners start to enter this night shortly after the initial stages of their spiritual life.

Chapter 9

Signs for Discernment

Difficulties in spiritual exercises and dryness in beginners does not necessarily proceed from the dark night. It can also come from weakness, imperfection, bodily indisposition or lukewarmness. There are three principal signs for knowing whether these difficulties proceed from the dark night of purgation. The first sign is that since these souls do not get satisfaction from the things of God, they do not get any from creatures either. They do not find delight in anything. If this dryness were not the authentic dark night of the senses, but came from carelessness or weakness, there would still be an attraction to things of the senses.

A second sign or condition is also necessary because the want of satisfaction in earthly or heavenly things could come from some indisposition, physical or psychological. The soul thinks that it is not serving God because of this distaste for the things of God whenever it tries to turn its attention to God. It is concerned and pained about this. Lukewarm people would not be concerned. The genuine purgative dryness may be furthered by some psychological or physical ailment such as an operation or the death of a family member or the loss of a job, etc. Indeed, this is often the case. Still, it does not fail to produce its purgative effect on the sensible appetite.

The reason for this spiritual dryness is that God is transferring his goods and strength from sense to spirit. Now the spirit is tasting but the senses are not. The spirit grows stronger and becomes more solicitous than ever about not failing God. At first, the soul does not experience any spiritual delight because it is accustomed to sensory feelings, and it lacks the gratification it formally enjoyed so readily. This will be remedied gradually by means of the dark night in which the beginnings of contemplation will occur. This will be hidden from the soul but will give it, together with the dryness in the senses, an inclination toward solitude. However, the soul will be unable to dwell on any particular thought nor will it desire to do so. This is the contemplative experience. The soul will be, as it were, in idleness without care for any interior or exterior work. While remaining quiet and without care for anything, the soul will soon experience interior nourishment. As one writer puts it, "The soul must persevere in this nothingness and nowhere until he finds joy in this contemplation."

In this state of contemplation, the soul has left discursive meditation and in this new state it is God who works in it. The intellect is left no support and the will no satisfaction and the memory no remembrance. The soul's personal efforts are useless and even an obstacle. The fruit of this contemplation is quiet, solitary and peaceful, and far removed from the sensible gratification of beginners.

The third sign for the discernment of this purgation of the senses is the inability of the soul to meditate or make use of the imagination as was its custom. God does not communicate himself now through the senses by means of discursive analysis but through an act of simple contemplation. There is no thought or memory whatsoever.

Chapter 10

The Conduct Required of Souls in this Dark Night

It is at the time of the dryness of the dark night of the senses that God brings the soul from meditation to contemplation. Here, the soul no longer has the power to meditate with its faculties on the things of God. Spiritual persons thus fear they have gone astray since they find no satisfaction in good things. They strive, as was their custom, to concentrate their faculties with some satisfaction on discursive meditation. Otherwise, they feel that they are doing nothing. This effort interferes with God's work in their soul. If they do not have adequate spiritual direction, they may hinder progress or lose courage. Meditation is useless for them because God is conducting them along another road, which is contemplation. They must trust in God patiently and persevere with a simple heart. He will bring them to that clear light by means of another dark night.

Those in the dark night of the senses should pay no attention to discursive meditation but allow their souls to remain in rest even though it may seem that they are wasting time. They are being brought to a freedom of soul which will liberate them from the impediment and fatigue of ideas and thoughts. They must now be content with a loving and peaceful attentiveness to God without the desire to taste or feel him. Contemplation is a peaceful quiet and sweet idleness of the soul. The soul should endure peacefully scruples about the loss of time and the value of activity.

The soul should not mind if the operation of their faculties are being lost to them. God is bestowing upon them infused contemplation to make room in the spirit for that great love that this dark and secret contemplation will bring.

CHAPTER 11

GOD'S WORK CONTINUES

There is an intense form of love that belongs to contemplation that is not found at the beginning owing to the impurity of the sensory part of the soul. Also because the soul, for want of understanding, has not made within itself a peaceful place for it. From time to time, however, the soul will begin to feel a certain longing for God without understanding whence it comes. It can even occasionally become very intense.

It is good to repeat that individuals generally do not receive this love in the beginning but rather experience a dryness and emptiness. This is often accompanied by a solicitude for God and a grief or fear about not serving him. This is not a servile fear but a reverential one and very pleasing to God. The soul is now, in spite of its aridity and emptiness, beginning to experience the elimination of many imperfections and the acquisition of many virtues. This enables it to receive a deeper experience of love. Remember that God is introducing the soul into this night to purge the senses and to subject and unite the lower part of the soul to the upper or spiritual part. This involves a cessation of discursive meditation. It is usually not apparent at the time but this results in many benefits. This departure from the bonds of the senses is a sheer grace.

The soul, while subject to the senses, was seeking God through feeble, limited, error-prone operations. We spoke of these earlier in relation to the seven capital vices found in beginners. The dark night is now freeing the soul from these vices by quenching its earthly and even heavenly satisfaction. Discursive meditations are difficult or even impossible but many other virtues and goods are acquired. It is good for the soul who treads this difficult path to know that it engenders many blessings. These blessings come about when, by means of this dark night, the soul departs from created things and walks toward eternal things. It is a narrow gate and many are called to enter through it. Unfortunately, not many respond to this call.

In this dark night the soul becomes grounded in faith which is not compatible with the sensible appetites. It is this faith, when purified, that will allow the soul to enter the second dark night, the night of the spirit.

~

CHAPTER 12

BENEFITS OF THE NIGHT OF THE SENSES

B ecause of the many benefits the soul gains through this dark night, it can also be called a glad night. Having been weaned from baby's milk, the soul is beginning to taste the food of the strong—that is, infused contemplation. The chief benefit of this dark night is the knowledge of self and of one's own wretchedness. The dryness of the faculties in relation to the abundance previously experienced makes the soul able to recognize its own lowliness. This was not apparent in the time of its prosperity. This self-knowledge is the virtue of humility wherein the soul recognizes itself to be nothing and finds no satisfaction in self because it is aware that of itself it neither does not can do anything. This results in a feeling of dejection because the soul becomes convinced that if it is doing nothing, it is not serving God at all. This self-knowledge or humility becomes the fountain of many more benefits.

The first benefit is that the soul communes with God with greater respect. Another benefit resulting from this dark night of purgation is not only a knowledge of the soul's own misery and loneliness but also a knowledge of God's grandeur and majesty. Self-knowledge—that is, humility— is foundational to knowledge of God. St. Augustine said to God: "Let me know myself, Lord, and I will know you." The spiritual humility that comes by means of this self-knowledge purges the soul from the imperfections stemming from pride which it experienced in its time of consolations. They are delivered from the temptation to see themselves as better than others.

From this stems love of neighbor because they esteem others rather than judge them. They are so aware of their own misery, they have no opportunity to watch anyone else's conduct. These souls also become submissive and obedient in the spiritual journey. The awareness of their own wretchedness prompts them not only to listen to other's teachings but even to desire direction from them.

~

Chapter 13

More Benefits

In this obscure night, the soul is reformed in its imperfections of avarice. Formally the gratification it found in spiritual things made them crave even more so that it was never content. Now it finds these practices distasteful and difficult, hence uses them more moderately. The lack of gratification helps the soul become detached. The soul is also freed from spiritual lust because these impurities ordinarily proceed from the delight taken on a sensible level. The soul no longer has this delight.

Spiritual gluttony is curbed. The sensual appetites are curbed through this dark night and so are brought into subjection. As a result, the passions lose their strength from not receiving any satisfaction. Further benefits proceed from this. The soul is able to dwell in spiritual peace and tranquility because there is no disturbance from concupiscence and the sensible appetites. The soul is given an habitual remembrance of God, accompanied by a fear of turning back on the spiritual road. Another benefit for the soul in this night is that it exercises all the virtues together. The soul practices the love of God without consolation since it is no longer motivated by the gratification it found previously. The soul also becomes charitable toward others. This will lessen the vice of envy and, if any remains, it will be a holy envy, desirous of imitating the virtues of others. Sloth and weariness are moderated as God takes from the soul its satisfaction in sensible things.

In the midst of these trials, God frequently communicates to the soul, when least expected, a spiritual sweetness, a pure love and spiritual knowledge. This is done with extreme delicacy apart from the senses and, in the beginning, the soul is hardly aware of its value. Insofar as the soul is purged of its sensory affections, it obtains freedom of spirit in which is acquired the 12 fruits of the Holy Spirit. The soul is also wondrously freed from the world, the flesh and the devil because these things require sensory gratification to operate on the soul. The soul is now able to walk with purity in the love of God, lacking the presumptuousness and self-satisfaction it previously had. This results in the holy fear that preserves and gives increase to the virtues.

In this dry night solicitude for God and longings about serving him increase. The soul has calmed the passions through mortification and lulling to sleep the natural sensory appetites. This results in harmony and peace in the interior senses.

Chapter 14

The Illuminative Way

When the senses are stilled, the passions quenched, and the appetites calmed by the purgation of the senses, the soul then enters into the way of proficients, the Illuminative Way. This is the way of infused contemplation. God himself refreshes the soul without its own active help or discursive meditation. This is the night of the senses. It is usually accompanied by trials and temptations that may last a long time. It is a preliminary to the night of the spirit and, for those called eventually to this spiritual purgation, the trials are similar. Strong sexual temptations are apt to occur during this difficult time. The imagination can be afflicted with a blasphemous spirit, scruples, and difficulties of faith. The senses and faculties are being prepared to enter into the night of the spirit and the wisdom that is found there. The Wise Man says: "He who is not tempted, what does he know? And he who is not tried, what are the things he knows?" By these trials the soul is truly humbled in preparation for its exultation. The period of time for these trials differs with different souls. The temptations also differ according to the amount of imperfections that must be purged from each one. Also according to the measure of love to which God wishes to raise a soul, he humbles it with greater or less intensity, or for a longer or shorter period of time.

Those who have a more considerable capacity and strength for suffering, God purges more intensely and quickly. The weak are usually kept in this night for a longer time. Their purgation is less intense and God frequently refreshes their senses to help them persevere. They may reach the blessed union of the Unitive Way late in life or they may never reach it entirely because they are never completely in this night or out of it. To keep them in humility and self-knowledge, God may exercise them for short periods in temptations and aridities. At other times he comes to their aid to encourage them. Souls who will pass on to the happy and lofty state which is the blessed union of love must usually remain in these temptations for a long time. We will now begin our consideration on this second night.

~

THE DARK NIGHT OF THE SOUL
BOOK TWO

CHAPTER 1

THE DARK NIGHT OF THE SPIRIT

When God intends to lead the soul eventually to a state of perfection in this life, he does not put it in the dark night of the spirit right after it is delivered from the trials of the night of the senses. The soul usually spends many years exercising itself in the state of proficients, in the Illuminative Way. The soul finds a serene, loving contemplation in its spirit without the use of discursive meditation. Yet, certain needs, aridities, darknesses, and conflicts are felt. They are more intense than those difficulties of the past. They are messengers of the coming night of the spirit, but are not as lasting as they will be in that night.

In the Illuminative Way the trials last for only short periods of time or for a few days and then it immediately returns to its customary serenity. In this way God purges some souls (proficients) who are not destined to ascend to the Unitive Way. These trials though are never as intense as the trials will be for those who are called to be perfect.

CHAPTER 2

IMPERFECTIONS OF PROFICIENTS

The imperfections of proficients are either habitual or actual. Habitual imperfections are the result of the inability of the sensory purgation to reach the spirit. Sensory purgations cut a plant off at the surface but do not pull up the roots. They serve more for the accommodation of the senses to the spirit than for the union of the spirit with God. The stains of the old self still linger though they may not be perceptible. They must be wiped away if the soul is to reach the purity of divine union. The souls of proficients still have the natural dullness contracted by sin and inattentive spirit. The hardships and conflicts of the night of the spirit will illumine, clarify, and recollect.

Imperfections of proficients may also be what is known as actual. These differ among souls considerably. They involve an abundance of spiritual communications in the sensory and spiritual parts of the soul, including imaginative and spiritual visions. These souls can often be tricked by the flesh and the devil. They must renounce all of these experiences and energetically defend themselves through faith.

In this stage the souls may be induced into believing vain visions and false prophecies. They are then filled with presumption and pride. They allow themselves to be seen in exterior acts of apparent holiness, such as raptures and other displays. They abandon holy fear which is the guardian of all the virtues. These imperfections belong to the lower part of the soul and are not as intense, pure, and vigorous as those required for blessed union. What is required is that the soul must enter the second night of the spirit where both the sensory and spiritual parts are despoiled of all of these apprehensions and delight, and the soul is made to walk in dark, pure faith. That is why the soul must reject all of these illusory pleasures.

CHAPTER 3

WHAT FOLLOWS

The lower, sensual part of the soul has now been fed with sweet communications and can now be accommodated and united to the higher, spiritual part of the soul. Now the two parts of the soul, higher and lower, are united and conformed and prepared to suffer the rough purgation of the spirit that awaits them. The real purgation of the senses begins with the spirit. Hence the night of the senses should really be called a reformation and bridling of the appetite rather than a purgation, as we have been calling it. The disorders of the sensory part are rooted in the spirit and receive strength from it. Thus all good and evil habits reside in the spirit and unless these habits are purged, the senses cannot be completely purified.

So it is that in this night of the spirit, both parts are jointly purified. The purification of the first night allows the sensory part, united in a certain way with the spirit, to undergo purgation and suffering with great fortitude. The lower part would not have the fortitude needed to endure the night of the spirit if it had not undergone its earlier purgations and consolations.

Until the gold of the spirit is purified, proficients will still be very lowly and natural in their communion with God. Vis-á-vis God they are still like little children. They have not reach that union of the soul with God through which they will be fully grown. When they are fully grown, they will do mighty works since their faculties will be more divine than human at that point.

To be fully grown God must purify the faculties, affections, and senses, both spiritual and sensory, interior and exterior. He must leave the intellect in darkness, the will in dryness, the memory in emptiness, and the affections in affliction, bitterness, and anguish. He will do this by depriving the soul of the feeling and satisfaction it previously obtained from spiritual blessings. This is necessary if the spiritual form, the union of love, is to be introduced into the soul and united with it. The Lord works all of this in the soul by means of a pure and dark contemplation.

☙

CHAPTER 4

CONTEMPLATIVE PURGATION

With the intellect, will and memory darkened and afflicted by the purification of the first night, in the soul left in the darkness of pure faith, it is now able to depart from its low manner of understanding, its feeble way of loving and its poor and limited method of finding satisfaction in God. It can also do this unhindered by the world, the flesh or the devil.

The soul is now able to depart from its human operation and way of acting to God's operation and way of acting. The intellect changes from human and natural to divine. It no longer understands by means of its natural strength and light, but by means of divine wisdom to which it is united. The will also becomes divine and no longer loves in a lowly manner by natural strength but with the strength of the Holy Spirit. The memory, too, is changed into presentments of eternal glory. All the strengths and affections of the soul, by means of this night, are renewed with divine qualities and delights.

CHAPTER 5

AFFLICTION AND TORMENT

Infused contemplation is a term which is often misunderstood. It occurs at this point in this dark night when an inflow of God into the soul purges it of its habitual ignorance and imperfections, natural and spiritual. It is the loving wisdom of God which purges and gives light, thus preparing the soul for union through love. It is the same loving wisdom that illumines the spirits in heaven.

It is called a dark night even though it is a divine light. The divine wisdom surpasses the ability of the soul to understand. Just as the sun surpasses the ability of the eye to look directly at it but rather blinds it, so does this wisdom seem to darken the soul. This wisdom as well as being dark to the soul is painful and afflictive because of the soul's baseness.

So when the divine light of contemplation strikes a soul not yet completely purified, it causes spiritual darkness by surpassing the act of natural understanding. For this reason infused contemplation is called a "ray of darkness." In these beginnings this dark contemplation is also painful to the soul. Infused contemplation has many extremely good properties while the still unprepared soul has many extreme miseries. The divine light afflicts the soul not yet completely purged just as a bright light afflicts sickly and weak eyes. It seems to the soul that God has rejected it. The soul understands distinctly it is not worthy of God and feels it will never be worthy. Its mind is immersed in the knowledge and feeling of its own miseries. Because of the soul's natural, moral and spiritual weakness, it undergoes, in sense and spirit, such agony that it would consider death a relief. It is quite amazing that the hand of God, which is light and gentle, should feel so heavy. It does not press down or weigh on the soul but only touches it. It is God's aim to grant favors to the soul, not to chastise it.

Chapter 6

Further Afflictions

There are two powers, divine and human, which afflict the soul at this time. The divine power strikes in order to renew the soul and divinize it by stripping it of the habitual affections of the old self. It absorbs it, as it were, in a profound darkness so that the soul feels that it is undergoing a cruel, spiritual death. This is fitting because it will attain a spiritual resurrection.

The greatest suffering that the soul then feels is the conviction that God has rejected it. The soul feels unworthy of God and only fit for the sorrows of hell. The soul also feels forsaken even by friends. The soul also experiences an emptiness in regard to all temporal, natural, and spiritual goods. God is purging the soul, inside and out, leaving it in dryness and darkness. We call this a dark contemplation. As fire consumes the imperfections of metal, this dark contemplation annihilates, empties and consumes all the affections and imperfect habits of a lifetime. These imperfections are deeply rooted in the substance of the soul so it suffers a great inner torment. God is humbling the soul greatly in order to exalt it greatly afterwards. God limits the duration of these sufferings, usually for a few days and at intervals, according to the ability of the soul to bear them.

Chapter 7

Yet Further Afflictions

The afflictions which torment the soul undergoing these passive purifications are only increased by the memory of its past consolations. This purgation may last for years, depending upon the graces God wishes to bestow. It will, however, be alleviated now and then by periods of consolation. These periods will be so powerful that the soul will be convinced that they will never end. However, they will end and the soul will be equally convinced that the sufferings it then experiences will never end. Even a competent spiritual director will be unable to offer the soul comfort. It will think the director does not truly know how sinful it is, and how unworthy it is of God's love.

St. Theresa speaks of this experience. She says it is like the sun hiding itself for days behind a deep layer of dark clouds so cold and dreary that the soul thinks that the sun is gone forever. Then suddenly, without any effort on the soul's part, the clouds separate and the sun shines forth even more brilliantly and warmer than before. The clouds are forgotten and it seems that the sun will shine forever. But it does not. The darkness returns and the soul is equally convinced that it will never end. Julian of Norwich speaks of this experience as a series of miseries and consolations but that somehow God loves her as much in the one as in the other.

The Scriptures are filled with such descriptions. We see them very graphically in the Psalms, in the Book of Job, and in the Lamentations of Jeremiah. The soul is convinced that God does not love it and that it is so unworthy that no human could love it either. During this time the soul does not lack the habit of the virtues of faith hope and love but it does not experience them in any form of consolation. The soul is not aware that this suffering is simply the finger of God touching it in its innermost parts to make it more supple and pliant for a blessed union.

CHAPTER 8

FORGETFULNESS

This night purges the intellect of its light, and the will of its affections and the memory of its knowledge. It seems that the soul cannot pray in any way at all or, at best, only feebly. The soul can do nothing because God is working in it. The soul is no longer in charge. God is. Because the memory is so weakened, the soul often forgets matters both spiritual and temporal and finds it impossible to concentrate on any task at hand.

It seems, as it were, as though the memory has become annihilated. It is engulfed in this divine, dark, spiritual night of contemplative light and so is withdrawn from all creature affections. The stronger this spiritual light, the more it deprives and darkens the soul. The clearer supernatural things are in themselves, the darker they are to our intellects. When the divine ray of contemplation strikes the soul with its divine light, it surpasses all natural light and thereby darkens the soul of all its natural abilities and lights.

Because this divine light is so pure, it is unaffected by any particular intelligible object. Also because the faculties of the soul are empty and annihilated, it is able to perceive and penetrate anything, earthly or heavenly, that God presents to it. This is true wisdom. The soul, so purged of all particular knowledge, does not find satisfaction in anything in particular and, remaining in emptiness and darkness, embraces all things. As St. Paul says, "Having nothing, yet it possesses all things" (2 Cor. 6).

CHAPTER 9

DARKNESS OF INTELLECT AND WILL

This night darkens the spirit in order to give it light. It humbles souls and reveals their wretchedness in order to exalt them. It empties them of all natural affections so that they may reach out in grace to enjoy everything. This purity of the spirit allows divine wisdom to give it delight in all things, unhindered by natural affections. Attachment to even one particular object would hinder this experience. The divine light transcends natural light and cannot coexist in a soul attached to anything less than itself. This darkness will last as long as is needful for the annihilation of the intellect's habitual way of knowing.

The will also must be purged of all its affections and feelings if it is to experience the delicate affection of divine union. It is only after the expulsion of all its usual attractions that the will can be transformed by the divine touch because the eye has not seen nor ear heard, nor has it entered into the heart of humans, the delights of divine union. The divine experience that God wishes to give to the soul is foreign to its customary manner of human experience. Sometimes it seems to the soul that it is being taken out of itself by afflictions. These afflictions are really a new birth because, at times, they leave the soul charmed and filled with delights from the Holy Spirit.

The soul will be given a new delightful sense experience and knowledge of all human and divine realities. This will be something beyond its common experience and natural knowledge. This is the gift of wisdom, the ability to see, as it were, through the eyes of God. It can only be given, however, when the memory, intellect and will are purged and purified of every attachment to things less than God. The wisdom then given will indeed surpass all understanding. It will involve a peace which the world cannot give.

This night is painful and the soul undergoing it may even on occasion express its suffering vocally and through tears. This suffering is profound, intimate and penetrating and the love which follows it will be likewise. Contemplation, of itself, is a gracious gift from God and does not bestow pain but rather sweetness and delight. It is the weakness and imperfection of the soul that is responsible for the suffering element.

Chapter 10

A Comparison

The purification and loving knowledge (divine light) we are speaking of affects the soul the same way that fire affects a log. Fire dehumidifies the wood, dispelling all moisture. It then brings to light every dark and ugly aspect of the wood and even causes an unpleasant odor. Finally the fire transforms the wood into itself and makes it beautiful with its own beauty.

Passively, the wood now possesses the properties and activities of the fire. Yet, it is still a log of wood. It is dry and it dries. It is hot and it gives off heat. It is brilliant and it gives light. It is the fire that produces all of these qualities in the wood. This is how the divine, loving fire of contemplation transforms the soul. It stirs up and evaporates evil in the soul, even evil that the soul had not been aware of. They are now brought to light and clearly seen and may now be expelled. Actually, the soul still has the same relationship that it had with God before this purgation but its subjective feeling, now aware of its evil, is convinced that it is not only unworthy but deserving of God's wrath. This feeling does not come from God but from the soul's own feebleness.

When these imperfections are gone, the soul's suffering ends and only joy remains. Sometimes in this process the soul is given a respite so that it can be aware of what is happening in its own process of purification. In these intervals of joy, the soul is remotely aware that further purification remains. It does, and the soul, once again, feels that it will never be freed from its suffering. It is now time to leave these painful experiences and look at the fruit of the soul's suffering.

Chapter 11

The Fruit of the Dark Night

During these dark purgations, the soul feels that it is experiencing a strong, divine love which is a certain foretaste of God. At the same time, its intellect is in darkness. This is an infused love. It is consensual but more passive than active. It enters into some of the properties of union with God. God's love imparts strength, fire and passion. As all the appetites of the soul have been brought into subjection and are unable to be satisfied by anything less than God, God finds the soul equipped and able to receive, to some extent, divine union. The soul is able to love God with all its strength and all its sensory and spiritual appetites. These appetites are no longer dissipated by other attachments.

Truly now the soul is able to love God with its whole heart, its whole mind, its whole soul, and all its strength. Yet with all this, the soul is still in darkness and doubt.

The soul's desire for God's love is increased in a thousand ways but it still suffers. There seems to be no place for the soul within itself, in heaven or on earth. All is darkness. The modality of supernatural hope still remains but it is without comfort. Isaiah explains this when he says: "My soul desired you in the night and until the morning, I will watch for you" (chapter 26). Desire and anxiety for love in the innermost parts of the spirit becomes a way of suffering. This gives the soul a certain inner strength but when the anxious, dark desire passes the soul often feels alone and weak. This is so because that inner strength of the dark fire of love is impressed on the soul passively and when this painful love ceases, so does this inner strength.

Chapter 12

Divine Wisdom

This dark night purifies the soul but it does so through love because this is the only way God acts. Perhaps this is what is sometimes known as "tough love." This dark contemplation gives the soul both love and wisdom according to its capacity and its need. Angels receive the wisdom of God and his love in sweetness and light because they are pure spirits and this is their mode of being. Men and women, however, receive wisdom and light through darkness in anguish because of their feebleness. Through a gradual puri- fication, they become capable of receiving this love and wis- dom in tranquility.

The purifying fire of love first dries out and prepares the wood, which is the soul. Then gradually the fire begins to give off the warmth of love. This divine fire of love burns in the will and, at the same time, communicates wisdom to the intellect. Sometimes it is felt in the will alone as love. At other times it is felt in the intellect alone as wisdom.

CHAPTER 13

FURTHER EFFECTS OF THIS DARK NIGHT

This dark contemplation of the night of the spirit some- times illumines the intellect with wisdom and some- times inflames the will with love. Now the one, then the other. St. Teresa of Avila says that a person can be so con- fused that one does not even know how one feels. The more common experience, however, is an inflaming of love in the will, rather than a deepening of understanding in the intel- lect. This inflaming of love comes from God exclusively by enkindling the appetite of the will. It is a sheer grace that the will passively receives.

The will requires less purging to receive the passion of love then the intellect does to receive the experience of wis- dom. Thus the love is received sooner and more frequently.

This is a spiritual fire and a spiritual thirst of love. It is much more intense than the enkindling of love we have seen in the night of the senses. Correspondingly the suffering of this purgation is proportionately greater than the suffering experienced in the night of the senses. From the beginning of this night of the spirit, the soul is touched with urgent longings of love, going from lesser to greater. The greatest fear the soul has is that God has been lost and has abandon it. These longings for God are so great that these souls usually acquire unusual strength and courage to do anything they deem necessary to encounter this God whom they love. Nothing seems impossible to them and they cannot conceive that anybody else would feel otherwise. Like a lion or a she-bear searching for lost cubs at night, the soul rises up and anxiously goes out in search of God. Immersed in darkness, it feels that it is dying of love. With the strength bestowed by love, the soul hungers for the perfection of love in divine union. Yet the soul still feels unworthy and miserable because its intellect is not yet illumined.

It is worth repeating that the suffering the soul experiences here does not come from God but only from the weaknesses of the soul. God has been giving light to the soul from the beginning but it could only see what is nearest to itself—namely, its own darknesses and miseries. Once this nearsightedness is expelled by the purging's of this dark night, the immense benefits acquired will begin to appear. The intellect and the will become illumined with supernatural light, united with the divine. A divine conversion takes place changing the memory, the affections and the appetites according to God. The soul becomes more divine than human. Again, all of this is sheer grace!

CHAPTER 14

FREEDOM FROM LOWER OPERATIONS

This dark night in which the soul is now immersed puts to sleep the lower operations, passions and appetites. Otherwise they would be a continual hindrance to its union with God. The soul's natural activity hinders the reception of the spiritual goods from this union. God infuses into the soul his supernatural goods passively, secretly and silently while the lower activities of the soul are asleep. This good fortune can only be understood through experience. Through this experience the soul will realize how the life of the spirit is true freedom and wealth.

CHAPTER 15

GOOD RESULTS OF THE DARK NIGHT

The soul is in no danger of being lost because of the torments, the doubts and the fear of this darkness. In fact these very things work toward its salvation. The soul is operating through, in and with the supernatural virtue of faith. It is also secure because its appetites, affections and passions were put to sleep or mortified and no longer have power over him.

~

CHAPTER 16

SECURITY IN THIS DARK NIGHT

It is in order that the soul may be enlightened supernaturally that this night darkens the sensory, the interior and the spiritual appetites. They are no longer able to find pleasure in anything at all. The memory, the imagination and the intellect are darkened and unable to function. Over them hangs a dense and burdensome cloud ("the cloud of unknowing"). The soul walks securely in this cloud, freed from its appetites. They can no longer lead the soul into error or into the snares of the world, the flesh and the devil. The soul is subject now only to the blessings of union with God. It is no longer distracted with useless things. It is secure from vainglory, from presumption and from false joy. The soul, by walking in darkness, not only avoids losing its way but actually advances rapidly.

The faculties must be darkened even in relation to good, spiritual and holy things. This is so because, in themselves, the faculties can only operate according to their own nature and abilities. But these are incapable of lifting them up to God. Only God can lift them up to God. The soul should see this darkening experience then as a grace, not as an affliction. God is freeing the soul from itself. By faith, God is taking the soul by the hand and guiding it through the darkness to a place it knows not. What greater security could it have!

There is another reason by which the soul is secure in this darkness. The soul advances by suffering. Strength is given to the soul by God. The virtues are practiced, the soul is purified and blessed with wisdom. This obscure wisdom or "ray of darkness" immerses the soul into the dark night of contemplation, protects it, frees it from all that is not God and brings it ever closer.

By this dark contemplation, God cares for the soul like a good nurse cares for a sick person, carefully safeguarding it from all surrounding dangers. As we are told in Psalm 18, "God makes the darkness his hiding place." The light which is God blinds and darkens our natural faculties and, at the same time, protects them from the world, the flesh and the devil. The soul is also given a wonderful solicitude about what it should do or not do in the service of God so that the powers of the soul are used only in paying homage to God.

CHAPTER 17

SECRET WISDOM

By way of love this dark contemplation infuses into the soul a secret, dark wisdom. It is called secret and dark because it is not known to the intellect or our other faculties. This wisdom cannot be fathomed by the intellect or the world or the flesh or the devil since it is given directly by God. Thus it is protected from them all. This contemplation, or wisdom of love, communicates an illumination which is ineffable. The soul cannot adequately express it or describe it or communicate it in any way.

It is beyond the ability of the imaginative faculty to deal with it. It is so spiritual and intimate to the soul that it transcends everything sensory and even the ability of the exterior and interior senses. This results in the soul being so elevated and exalted that it sees every created thing as deficient and inadequate in dealing with this divine experience. The soul has been brought into the realm of mystical theology which is essentially dark and secret to all of its faculties and natural capacity.

CHAPTER 18

THE WORK OF THIS SECRET WISDOM

This secret wisdom is like a ladder which the soul climbs to get to the treasures of heaven. Like a ladder it goes up and down, up to God and down to self-humiliation. According to Proverbs the soul is humbled before it is exalted and it is exalted before it is humbled (chapter 18). Tempests and trials usually follow prosperity. Abundance and peace succeed misery and torment. Perfect love of God and contempt of self cannot exist without knowledge of God and knowledge of self. The former is exultation; the latter is humility. Like a ladder, or step by step, this secret knowledge both illumines and enamors the soul raising it up to God.

CHAPTER 19

STEPS ONE THROUGH FIVE

There are 10 steps on this mystical ladder of Divine love by which the soul ascends to God. In the first step the soul is lovesick, not unto death but unto the glory of God. The soul loses its appetite for all created things. It is a form of annihilation where the soul becomes unable to find satisfaction or consolation in anything.

In the second step the soul relentlessly searches for God paying heed to nothing else. In everything that it does, the soul turns to its beloved. It is convalescing and gaining strength.

In Psalm 112 we read: "Blessed are they who fear the Lord, because in his commandments they long to work." This is the third step of this loving ladder, fervor in good works. Love makes long, hard and many works seem like short, easy and few. On this step of the mystical ladder, the soul sees itself as an unprofitable servant and worse than all others. Such a soul can say with all sincerity that it is the greatest sinner in all the world.

The fourth step on this ladder of love makes all burdensome and heavy things light. There is great energy on this step that brings the flesh under control. The soul asks nothing from God and is concerned only with rendering him service because of his favors. Personal interests are set aside. Favors from God are used only in his service. This is a very elevated step where suffering is inspired by love and where God often gives it the joy of spiritual delight.

The fifth step on the ladder of love bestows upon the soul a great longing for God. Even the slightest delay is intolerable to the soul who must see its loving God or die.

Chapter 20

Steps Six to Ten

On the sixth step of this ladder of love the soul runs swiftly toward God invigorated by love and strengthened by hope. The soul is almost completely purified and runs in the way of God's commandments. On the seventh step, love makes the soul bold. It believes all things, hopes all things, endures all things. The soul prays that God might kiss it with the kiss of his lips and boldly delights in God who will grant whatever it asks.

In the eighth step of love, the soul clings to God. For short periods of time the soul's desire for union is satisfied. Then comes the step of the perfect, the ninth step of the ladder of love. The soul is inflamed by the fire of the Holy Spirit by reason of its union with God. It is difficult to speak of this experience. The tenth step assimilates the soul to God completely and the soul departs from the body. Purged through love, the soul goes directly to the presence of God and by participation becomes God. This is total assimilation wherein the soul has departed from itself and from all things and ascends to God.

CHAPTER 21

FAITH, HOPE AND LOVE

The three theological virtues, faith, hope and love, protect the soul against its adversaries, the devil, the world and the flesh. They also prepare the soul for the union of the three faculties—intellect, memory and will—with God.

Faith renders the intellect sightless. Faith gives the soul more protection against the devil than all the other virtues. Faith is the foundation of all the virtues. It was by faith that the soul was able to walk, faithful to its beloved, without the comfort of intellectual light and without satisfaction from its spiritual teachers into interior darkness.

The virtue of hope defends and frees the soul from itssecond enemy, the world. Hope elevates the soul to things eternal and makes all earthly things seemed dead and worthless. It looks at God and receives from him all it needs. In God alone is it at rest.

The third supernatural virtue, charity, makes the soul beautiful and pleasing to God. It receives from God protection from its third enemy, the flesh. Where there is true love of God, love of flesh finds no place. Charity makes the other virtues genuine and strengthens them. It fortifies the soul and bestows on it loveliness and charm so as to please God. The three theological virtues have as their function the withdrawing of the soul from all that is less than God. Consequently their role is to join the soul with God.

Chapter 22

Hope and Encouragement

Liberated from the devil, the world and the flesh, the soul goes from the lowly to the sublime; from being earthly to heavenly; from being human to divine. Many souls pass through this night but do not understand it. They especially do not understand the blessings that it brings. We have written of these blessings to encourage souls frightened by so many trials for truly this night is a sheer grace for the soul.

Chapter 23

Protection from Evil

The darkness of this deep contemplation which the soul receives passively from God is protected from evil influences. The world the flesh and the devil can only affect the sensory part of the soul. The more spiritual and interior the communication from God is and the more removed it is from the senses, the less the powers of evil perceive or understand it.

The sensory part of the soul, which can be influenced by the world, the flesh and the devil, does receive a great quietude and silence from these deep interior communications. Consequently these evil powers, knowing the blessings God is bestowing, can indirectly disturb the sensory part with great suffering and fears. This causes the soul to enter more deeply into its inner depths where peace and joy increases and where fear is absent. Sometimes the spiritual communication from God is not bestowed exclusively on the spirit but on the senses, too, and great torment can result. The soul can receive true visions of Christ and, at the same time, false visions. This results in a spiritual suffering which, fortunately, does not last long as the soul could not handle it. It is allowed to happen so that the soul can be purified and prepared for even greater blessings. It is to God alone that all hearts lie open and there is a depth of spiritual communication coming directly from God that cannot be touched by any form of evil. The soul becomes completely spiritual, the passions and spiritual appetites are greatly eliminated and the soul is at peace.

Chapter 24

Rest and Divine Union

When the soul is at rest in all its appetites and faculties, then it is able to go out to divine union with God through love. God touches the soul, purifies, quiets, and strengthens it that she may receive the divine union permanently. This union can only be reached through a marvelous purity and this purity requires vigorous mortification.

Chapter 25

Conclusion

In this happy, contemplative night, God directs the soul in a secret way, so remote and alien to the senses, that nothing sensible or relating to creatures can detain her in her journey to union of love. Because of the spiritual darkness of this night all the powers of the soul are in obscurity and inoperable and cannot interfere with divine union. In addition, the soul has no support from the intellect. Love alone is what guides and moves her.

About the Publisher

LANTERN BOOKS was founded in 1999 on the principle of living with a greater depth and commitment to the preservation of the natural world. In addition to publishing books on animal advocacy, vegetarianism, religion, and environmentalism, Lantern is dedicated to printing books in the United States on recycled paper and saving resources in day-to-day operations. Lantern is honored to be a recipient of the highest standard in environmentally responsible publishing from the Green Press Initiative.

www.lanternbooks.com

CPSIA information can be obtained at www.ICGtesting.com
Printed in the USA
BVOW02s2048030914

365213BV00001B/1/P